Ch. Ph. Reiff

Little Manual of the Russian Language

A work in which the Russian words are represented with their

pronunciation figured in English characters and their accentuation

Ch. Ph. Reiff

Little Manual of the Russian Language
*A work in which the Russian words are represented with their pronunciation figured
in English characters and their accentuation*

ISBN/EAN: 9783337297916

Printed in Europe, USA, Canada, Australia, Japan

Cover: Foto ©Andreas Hilbeck / pixelio.de

More available books at **www.hansebooks.com**

OF THE

RUSSIAN LANGUAGE

A WORK

IN WHICH THE RUSSIAN WORDS ARE REPRESENTED
WITH THEIR PRONUNCIATION FIGURED IN ENGLISH CHARACTERS
AND WITH THEIR ACCENTUATION

BY

CH. PH. REIFF

THIRD EDITION, REVISED AND CORRECTED

PARIS

MAISONNEUVE AND Cᵒ, PUBLISHERS

15, QUAI VOLTAIRE, 15

1869

LITTLE

RUSSIAN MANUAL,

FOR THE USE OF THE ENGLISH.

ALPHABET AND PRONUNCIATION.

FORM OF THE LETTERS		PRONUNCIATION.	FORM OF THE LETTERS.		PRONUNCIATION.
Roman.	Italic.		Roman.	Italic.	
А, а.	*А, а.*	ah, a.	Т, т.	*Т, m.*	t.
Б, б.	*Б, б.*	b.	У, у.	*У, у.*	oo.
В, в.	*В, в.*	v.	Ф, ф.	*Ф, ф.*	f, ph.
Г, г.	*Г, i.*	g, gh.	Х, х.	*Х, x.*	kh, ch.
Д, д.	*Д, д.*	d.	Ц, ц.	*Ц, ц.*	ts.
Е, е.	*Е, е.*	yai *or* ai.	Ч, ч.	*Ч, ч.*	ch, tch.
Ж, ж.	*Ж, ж.*	zh.	Ш, ш.	*Ш, ш.*	sh.
З, з.	*З, з.*	z.	Щ, щ	*Щ, щ.*	sh-tch.
И, и.	*И, и.*	ee.	Ъ, ъ.	*Ъ, ъ.*	*mute* e.
I, i.	*I, i.*	ee.	Ы, ы.	*Ы, ы.*	we, ee *hollow*.
К, к.	*К, к.*	k.	Ь, ь.	*Ь, ь.*	*short* e.
Л, л.	*Л, л.*	l.	Ѣ, ѣ.	*Ѣ, ѣ.*	yai *or* ai.
М, м.	*М, м.*	m.	Э, э.	*Э, э.*	ai.
Н, н.	*Н, н.*	n.	Ю, ю.	*Ю, ю.*	you, ew.
О, о.	*О, о.*	o *or* ah.	Я, я.	*Я, я.*	yah.
П, п.	*П, п.*	p.	Ѳ, ѳ.	*Ѳ, ѳ.*	f, ph.
Р, р.	*Р, р.*	r.	Ѵ, ѵ.	*Ѵ, ѵ.*	e.
С, с.	*С, с.*	*hard* s *or* ss.	Й, й.	*Й, й.*	*short* e.

Observation. In the preceding alphabet, the characters г, х, е, щ, ѣ, ы, ь, ѣ, я, о, й, are the only letters whose pronunciation offers any difficulty.

Г has a sound nearly similar to that of *g*, in the English word *goose*, as in груша, *a pear*; read *groòsha*. But it has a guttural sound, not to be found in English, and which nearly resembles that of the German ф. This sound is especially perceivable in the middle of a word, when the r is followed by a consonant, also at the end of a word, as in Богъ, *God;* ногти, *the nails;* read *boф, nòфtee.* In inflections *аго, яго, ого, его* of adjectives and pronouns, the letter г is pronounced as *v;* as in краснаго, *of beautiful;* сйняго, *of blue;* одного, *of one;* его, *of him;* read *kràsnavah, seènyavah, adnavò, yaivò.*

Е has three different sounds:

1. This letter at the beginning of words purely Russian, and in all syllables in which it is preceded by a vowel, has a sound similar to that of *yai,* when the *y* is nearly sunk in the pronunciation, as in ему, *to him;* великое, *great;* read *yaimoò, vaileèkoyai.* — 2. At the beginning of words from foreign languages, and at the middle and end of a word, when preceded by a consonant, it has the sonnd of *e* in *met,* as in дерево, *a tree;* берегу, *I guard;* read *dayrevo, bayregoỏ.* — 3. In the termination *екъ* of diminutives, in all the characteristic inflections of cases in the nouns, and of persons in the verbs, finally in almost all words, this letter when accented has a sound nearly similar to that of short *yo* or *o;* as in кулекъ, *a little sack;* огнемъ, *by the fire;* ведёшь, *thou leadest;* медъ, *the honey;* шелкъ, *silk;* лицé, *the face;* read *koolyòk, agnyòm, vaidyòsh, myott, sholk, leetsò.* This sound *yo* or *o* of the letter *e* is commonly distinguished

by a diæresis over the vowel, as кулёкъ, огпёмъ, ведёшь, мёдъ, шёлкъ, лпцё.

X corresponds to the German ф. No sound can exactly represent its pronunciation. It is a strong aspiration that nearly resembles the sound *k* would have when pronounced hastily from the throat; as in хвалá, *the praise;* read *khvahláh.*

Щ unites the sound of *ш* and *ч*, as in щитъ, *the shield;* read *shtcheet.*

Ъ. — This letter has no sound whatsoever; it only serves to point out that the preceding consonant ought to be pronounced with greater effort, as it were doubled, as in глазъ, *the eye;* бобъ, *a bean;* ровъ, *a ditch;* родъ, *kind;* мужъ, *the husband;* read *glass, bopp, roff, rott, moosh.*

Ы has a hollow sound, nearly similar to that of the English *we*, when the *w* is pronounced rapidly; as in бýквы, *the letters,* read *boòkwe.* It has this sound after the consonants б, в, м, п, ф; but after another consonant, it is a thick *e*, as in сынъ, *the son;* read *seen.*

Ь. — This letter at the end of a word has a sound nearly similar to that of the very short *e*. When followed by a consonant in the middle of a word, it is mute; it is pronounced when followed by a vowel; as in знать, *to know;* мáленькій, *little;* здорóвье, *health;* read *znaht, màhlenkee, zdahròvyai.*

Ѣ at the beginning of a word has the sound of *yai;* as in ѣсть, *to eat;* read *yaist.* In the middle of a word it is also pronounced *yai*, when the sound of *y* is almost sunk; as in нѣтъ, *no;* read *nyaitt.* At the end of a word, this letter has the sound of *ay;* as in на столѣ, *on the table;* read *nah stahlay.*

Я has the following sounds. This vowel, when accented, has the sound of the diphthong *yah;* as in яма, *a pit;* мясо, *meat;* read *yàhmah, myàhso.* But if not accented, it is pronounced *yai,* as in ядро́, *a ball;* read *yaidrò.* The pronoun ея́, *of her,* is pronounced *yaiyò* and the syllable ся of pronominal verbs is pronounced *sah,* as in стара́ться, *to exert one's self;* боя́ться, *to fear;* read *stahràtsah, bahyàtsah.*

О is pronounced as English *o;* but if unaccented, it takes the sound of *ah,* as in ко́локолъ, *a bell;* колокола́, *bells;* read *kòlahkall, kahlakahlà.*

Й is a short *e,* which is pronounced very rapidly, as in дай, *give;* пей, *drink;* read *dahee* or *die, pey,* giving utterance to a short *e* after the vowel.

In general the pronunciation of Russian words depends especially upon the tonic accent, which is no longer printed in Russian books, except to distinguish some homonymous words, or some grammatical inflections of similar forms; as за́мокъ, *a castle,* and замо́къ, *a lock;* сло́ва, *of the word,* and слова́, *the words;* read *zàhmok* and *zahmòk, slòvah* and *slahvàh.* It is here the place to observe that in the Russian language there is no rule by which to determine the accent, and that in one and the same word it is frequently shifted from one syllable to another; for which reason all the words used in this Manual are printed with the accent they ought to have.

SELECTION

OF WORDS MOST FREQUENTLY MADE USE OF

IN CONVERSATION.

God and the objects relating to divine worship.

God,	Богъ,	Bokh.
faith, belief,	вѣра,	vairah.
religion, (law),	законъ,	zakòn.
worship,	богослуженіе,	bogosloozhènceyay.
the sermon,	проповѣдь,	pròpovaid.
an image,	икона,	eekòna.
the cross,	крестъ,	kraist.
holy water,	святая вода,	svaitàya vadàh.
the mass,	обѣдпя,	abaìdnya.,
the vespers,	вечерпя,	vaitchaìrnya.
a preacher,	проповѣдникъ,	propovaìdnik.
a priest,	священникъ,	svyastchènnik,
	(попъ),	(pop).
a christian,	христіанинъ,	khreestyànin.
a catholic,	католикъ,	katòlik.
a lutherian,	лютеранинъ,	lyoutairànin.
a reformer,	реформатъ,	raiformàt.
boliday,	праздникъ,	pràhznik.
a fast day,	постный депь,	pòssnee den.
an angel,	ангелъ,	ànghel.
the devil,	діаволъ,	dyàvoll.

6

Dignities, professions and trades.

The Emperor,	Императоръ, (Царь, Государь),	Impairàhtor, (tsar, gossoodàr).
the Empress,	Императрица, (Царица, Государыня),	Impairàhtreetsa, (tsareètsa, gossoodàhreenya).
the Grand-Duke,	Великій Князь,	vaileékee knyaz.
the Grand Duchess,	Великая Княгиня,	vaileékaya knyagheènya.
the King,	Король,	karòl.
the Queen,	Королёва,	karalaívah.
a Prince,	Князь,	knyaz.
a Princess,	Княгиня,	knyagkeènya.
(unmarried),	Княжна,	knyazhnà.
an Earl,	Графъ,	graff.
a Countess,	Графиня,	graffcénya.
a gentleman,	дворянинъ,	dvorainìn.
a citizen,	мѣщанинъ,	maistchanìn,
a peasant,	крестьянинъ, (мужикъ, vulg.)	kraityàhnin, (moozhìk.
a merchant,	купецъ,	koopèts.
a haberdasher,	лавочникъ,	làhvoshnik.
a bookseller,	книгопродавецъ,	kneegoprodàhvets.
an artist,	художникъ,	khoodòzhnik.
a tradesman,	ремёсленникъ,	raimèslennik.
an interpreter,	переводчикъ,	perevòdtchik.
a brewer,	пивоваръ,	peevavàr.
a baker,	булочникъ,	boòlotchnik.
a butcher,	мясникъ,	myassnik.
a barrister,	стряпчій,	stryàptchee.
a bootmaker,	сапожникъ,	sapòzhnik,
a shoemaker,	башмачникъ,	bashmàshnik.
a washerwoman,	прачка,	pràtchkah
a sempstress,	бѣлошвейка,	bailoshvaìka.
an apothecary,	аптекарь,	aptaìkar.
a surgeon,	лекарь,	laìkar.
a broker,	маклеръ,	màhkler

a clerk,	прикащикъ,	preekàstchik.
a counsellor,	совѣтникъ,	savaìtnik.
a knight,	кавалеръ,	kavalèr.
a dentist,	зубной врачъ,	zoobnòy vratch.
a barber,	цырюльникъ,	tseeryoùlnik.
a comedian, actor,	актёръ,	aktyòr.
a musician,	музыкантъ,	moozeekànt.
a tailor,	портной,	partnòy.
a midwife,	повивальная бабка,	pavevàlnaya bàbka.
the servant, boy,	слуга, малый,	sloogàh, màhlee.
servant-maid, girl,	служанка, дѣвка,	sloozhànka, dyèvka.
a nurse,	кормилица, мамка,	karmeèlitsa, màmka.
serfs,	крѣпостные люди,	kraipossnyai lyoùdi.
an inn-keeper,	трактирщикъ,	trakteèrstchik.
a hackney-coach-man,	извощикъ,	eezvòstchik.
the porter,	дворникъ,	dvòrnik.
waterman, boatman,	перевозчикъ,	perevòstchik.
a watchman,	буточникъ,	boòtotchnik.
a foreigner,	иностранецъ,	eenastràhnets
a traveller,	приѣзжій,	preeyaizhee.
a beggar,	нищій,	neèstchee.

Military profession.

A fieldmarshal,	Фельдъ-маршалъ,	feldmàrshall.
a general,	генералъ,	gheneràll.
a major-general,	генералъ-маіоръ,	gheneràll-mayor.
an aid de camp,	адъютантъ,	adyoutànt.
an aid de camp of the sovereign,	флигель-адъю-тантъ,	fleèghel-adyoutànt.
a colonel,	полковникъ,	palkòvnik.
a lieutenant-colonel,	подполковникъ,	padpalkòvnik.
a major,	маіоръ,	mahyòr.
a captain of foot,	капитанъ,	kapeetàn.
a second captain,	штабсъ-капитанъ,	shtabs-kapeetàn.

a captain in a horse-regiment,	ро́тмистръ,	rótmeestr.
the commander of the garrison,	комендáнтъ,	komendànt.
a lieutenant,	порýчикъ,	paroòtchik.
a second lieutenant,	подпорýчикъ,	padparoòtchik.
an ensign,	прáпорщикъ,	pràhporstchik.
the sword,	шпáга,	shpàlıga.
the ensign, flag,	знáмя,	znàhmya.
the standard,	штандáртъ,	shtandàrt.
the spurs,	шпóры,	shpòree.
a gun,	ружьё,	ruozhyò.
the broad sword,	сáбля,	sàblya.
the ball,	пýля,	poòlia.
the cannon,	пýшка,	poòshka.
a cannon ball,	ядрó,	yaidrò.
the artillery,	артиллéрія,	artillairya.
the infantry,	пѣхóта,	paikhòtah.
the cavalry,	кóнница,	kònneetsa.
a sentinel, sentry,	часовóй, караýль-ный,	tchaissavòy, karaoòlnee.
the patrol,	дозóръ,	dazòr.
who goes there?	кто идётъ?	khto eedyòlt.
the war,	войнá,	vainàh.
the peace,	миръ,	meer.
the enemy,	непріятель,	nepreeyàhtel.
the native country,	отéчество,	alaìtchaistvo.
the wound,	рáпа,	ràhnah.

The town and the objects to be met with there.

The city, town,	гóродъ,	gòrot.
a suburb,	предмѣ́стіе,	predmaìstyai.
the fortress,	крѣ́пость,	kraìpost.
a palace,	дворéцъ,	dvarèts.
a market-town,	мѣстéчко,	maistaìtchko.
the exchange,	биржа,	beèrzha.
the church,	цéрковь,	tsaìrkov.

the theater,	теа́тръ,	taiàtr.
the hospital,	гошпита́ль,	goshpeetàll.
the town-house,	ра́туша,	ràhtoosha.
custom-house,	тамо́жня,	tamòzhnya.
the police,	поли́ція,	paleètsya.
the post-office,	по́чта,	pòtchtah.
a building,	зда́ніе,	zdàhnyai.
the admiralty,	адмиральте́йство,	admeeraltèistvo.
an inn,	тракти́ръ,	trakteèr.
a coffee-room,	кофе́йный домъ,	kafèinee dom.
a public house,	каба́къ,	kabàk.
a garden,	са́дъ,	sad.
a bridge,	мо́стъ,	most.
the street,	у́лица,	oòleetsa.
the foot-path,	тротуа́ръ,	trotooàr.
a blind alley,	глухо́й переу́локъ,	glookhòy pereoòlok.
the market,	ры́нокъ,	reènok.
the bazar,	гости́ный дворъ,	ghosteènee dvor.
a cross street,	переу́локъ,	pereoòlok.
the door,	дверь,	dvair.
a gate-way,	воро́та,	vahròtah.
the tower,	ба́шня,	bàshnya.
the river,	рѣка́,	raikàh.
the quay,	на́бережная,	nàberezhnaya.
the harbour,	га́вань, по́ртъ,	gàvan, port.
the promenade,	гульби́ще,	goolbeèstchai.
the prison,	тюрьма́,	tyourmàh.
a vessel, ship,	кора́бль,	karàbl.
a boat,	ло́дка, бо́тъ,	lòdkah, boat.
a steam-boat,	парохо́дъ,	parakhòt.
an island,	о́стровъ,	òstrof.
a wooden wall,	забо́ръ,	zahbòr.
the sea,	мо́ре,	mòrai.
the lake,	о́зеро,	òzairo.
the passage,	перее́здъ,	pereyàizd.
the voyage, journey,	путь,	poot.
a travelling-companion,	сопу́тникъ, попу́тчикъ,	sapoòtnik, papoòttchik.

The house and things connected with house-keeping.

The house,	домъ,	dom.
the yard,	дворъ,	dvor.
the room, chamber,	го́рнпца, ко́мната,	gȯrneetsa, kȯmnata,
	поко́й,	pakȯy.
the country house,	за́городный домъ,	zȧhgorodnee dom,
seat,	да́ча,	dȧtchah.
the stairs, the ladder,	ле́стнпца,	lȧisneetsa.
a bench,	скаме́йка, ла́вка,	skamėika, lȧfka.
a stove,	печь,	paitch.
hangings,	обо́п,	ahbȯee.
the plates and dishes,	посу́да,	passoȯda.
the chimney,	ками́нъ,	kamėn.
an ornamental clock,	сте́нны́е часы́,	stainnyai tchassė.
the water closet,	ну́жнпкъ,	noȯzhnik.
a chamber pot,	ури́льнпкъ,	ooreėlnik.
a chair,	сту́лъ,	stool.
a close stool,	су́дно,	soȯdno.
a cupboard,	шка́фъ,	shkaf.
a bedstead,	крова́ть,	kravȧt.
a bed,	посте́ль,	pastail.
a cushion, bolster,	поду́шка,	padoȯshka.
the bed-clothes,	одъя́ло,	adaiyȧlo.
blanket,		
a sheet,	простыня́,	prasteenyȧh.
a chest,	сунду́къ,	soondoȯk.
the window,	окно́, око́шко,	aknȯ, akȯshko.
the shutters,	ста́вни,	stȧvnee.
a wash-stand,	рукомо́йникъ,	rookamȯynik.
a towel,	полоте́нце, утп-	palatėntso ootee-
	ра́льнпкъ,	rȧlnik.
the soap,	мы́ло,	muėlo.
a mattress,	тюфя́къ,	tyoufyȧk.
the kitchen,	ку́хня,	koȯkhnya.
the woman-cook,	куха́рка,	kookhȧrka.
the cook, man-cook,	по́варъ,	pȯvar.

the fire,	огонь,	agòn.
fire-wood, fuel,	дрова,	dravàh.
the tender-box,	трутница, огпѝво,	troòtnitsa, agneèvo.
a candle,	свѣча,	svaitchà.
a candlestick,	подсвѣчпикъ,	padsvaitchnik,
	шапдалъ,	shandàll.
the key,	ключъ,	klyoutch.
a wax candle,	восковая свѣча,	vaskavàya svaitchà.
a looking-glass,	зеркало,	zèrkalo.
a screen,	ширмы,	sheèrmuee.
the coffee-pot,	коѳейпикъ,	kafèynik.
the toa-pot,	чайникъ,	tchàynik.
the tea-urn,	самоваръ,	samavàr.
a tea-board,	подпосъ,	padnòss.
the boiler,	котёлъ,	katyòll.
a pan, earthen pan,	чаша,	tchàsha.
a cup,	чашка,	tchàshka.
a saucer,	блюдечко,	blyoùdetchko.
a pitcher,	кружка,	kroòshka.
the bottle,	бутылка,	booteèlka.
the cork,	пробка,	pròpka.
the cork-screw,	пробочпикъ,	pròboshnik.
a glass,	стакапъ,	stakàn.
a wine-glass,	рюмка,	ryoùmka.
a basket,	корзинка,	karzeèna.
the lantern,	ѳопарь,	fanàr.
the snuffers,	щипцы,	shtcheèptsee.
a box,	коробка,	karòpka.
a hammer,	молотокъ,	molotòk.
a funnel,	воропка,	varònka.
the brush,	щётка,	stchòtka.
the boot-jack,	служка,	sloòshka.
a comb,	гребень,	graiben.
the coach, carriage,	карета,	karaita.
the sledge,	сапи,	sànee.
the cellar,	погребъ,	pògreb.
a cask, tun,	бочка,	bòtchka.

Eating and drinking.

The meat, viands,	ку́шанья,	kooshanya').
the table-cloth,	ска́терть,	skàtert.
the knife,	ножъ, но́жикъ,	nosh, nòzhik.
the fork,	ви́лка,	veèlka.
a plate,	таре́лка,	taraìlka.
the napkin,	салфе́тка,	salfaìtka.
the spoon,	ло́жка,	lòshka.
the table-spoon,	супова́я ло́жка,	soopovàya lòshka.
the tea-spoon,	ча́йная ло́жка,	tchàynaya lòshka.
bread, some bread,	хлѣбъ, хлѣба,	khlaib, klaìba.
salt, some salt,	соль,	sol.
vinegar,	у́ксусъ,	oòksooss.
pepper,	пе́рецъ,	paìretse.
oil, olive-oil,	ма́сло, (деревя́нное ма́сло),	màslo, (derevyànnoyai màslo).
mustard,	горчи́ца,	gartcheètsa.
butter,	ма́сло, (коро́вье),	màslo, (karòvyai).
a slice of bread and butter,	хлѣбъ съ ма́сломъ,	khlaib s màslom.
meat,	мя́со,	myàhso.
beef,	говя́дина,	gavyàdeena.
veal,	теля́тина,	tailyàteena.
mutton,	бара́нина,	baràneena.
pork,	свини́на,	sveeneèna.
game,	дичи́на,	deetcheèna.
the breakfast,	за́втракъ,	zàftrak.
the dessert,	заку́ски,	zakoòskee.
the dinner,	обѣ́дъ,	abaid.
the supper,	у́жинъ,	oòzheen.
the soup,	су́пъ,	soop.
a cabbage-soup,	щи,	shtchee.
a fish-soup,	уха́,	ookhà.
a cold soup,	ботви́нья,	batveènya.
fish,	ры́бы,	reèbuee.
crayfish, crab, ·	ра́ки,	ràkee.
oisters,	у́стрицы,	oòstreetsee.

eggs,	яйца,	yàytsa.
caviar,	икра,	eekrà.
herring,	сельдь,	saild.
salmon,	сёмга,	syòmga.
potatoes,	картофель,	kartòfel.
a potato,	картофелина,	kartòfelecna.
an omelet,	яичница,	yaishnitsa.
pan-cakes,	блины,	bleeneè.
mushrooms,	грибы,	greebueè.
cucumbers,	огурцы,	agoortseè.
the cod-fish,	треска,	traiskà.
the lamprey,	минога,	meenòga.
vegetables,	зёлень,	zàilen.
beans,	бобы,	babueè.
onions,	луковицы,	loòkoveetsi.
peas,	горохъ,	garòkh.
cabbage,	капуста,	kapoòsta.
turnips,	рѣпа,	raìpa.
spinage,	шпинатъ,	shpeenàt.
garlick,	чеснокъ,	tchesnòk.
chitterlings,	колбасы,	kalbasseè.
horse-radish,	хрѣнъ,	khren.
meal,	мука,	mookà.
oat-meal, groats,	крупа,	kroopà.
gruel	каша,	kàsha.
cheese,	сыръ,	seer.
salad,	салатъ,	salàt.
asparagus,	спаржа,	spàrzha.
artichokes,	артишокп,	arteeshòkee.
biscuits,	сухари,	sookhareè.
ham,	окорокъ,	òkorok.
oranges,	апелсйны,	apelseènee.
strawberries,	земляника,	zemlaineèka.
garden strawberries,	клубника,	kloobneèka.
cherries,	вишпи,	veèshnee.
citrons, lemons,	лимоны,	leemònee.
nuts,	орѣхп,	araìkee.
coffee,	кофе,	kòfe.

tea,	чай,	tchaee.
milk,	молоко,	malakò.
the cream,	сливкп,	sleèfki.
the sugar,	сахаръ,	sàkhar.
the brandy,	водка,	vòtka.
the wine,	винò (рèнское),	veenò (rènskoyai).
the beer,	пиво,	peèvo.
punch,	пуншъ,	poonsh.
the water,	водà,	vadàh.

Dress and what serves for the toilet.

Clothes, dress,	одѣяніе, платье,	adaiyànyai, plàtyai.
a coat,	кафтанъ,	kaftàn.
the jacket,	камзолъ, жилéтъ,	kamzòll, zheelèt.
the doublet,	фуфайка,	foofàyka.
drawers,	подштанники,	padshtànneeki.
breeches, shorts	штаны,	shtànee.
pantaloons,	панталоны,	pantalònee.
stockings,	чулкй,	tchoolkeè.
a shirt, shift,	рубашка,	roobàshka.
a handkerchief,	платокъ носовой,	platòk nassavòy.
boots,	сапогй,	sapagheè.
slippers,	туфли,	toòflee.
a night-cap,	колпакъ,	kalpàk.
a cap,	шапка,	shàpka.
the hat,	шляпа,	shlyàhpa.
a cravat, neckcloth,	галстукъ,	gàlstook.
a neck handkerchief,	косынка,	kasscènka.
an apron,	переднпкъ,	perèdnik.
the gloves,	перчатки,	pertchàtkee.
the pocket,	карманъ,	karmàn.
a cloak,	епанчá, шппéль,	yaipàntcha, sheenèl.
a riding-coat,	сертукъ,	sertoòk.
a watch,	часы,	tchesseè.
the snuff-box,	табакéрка,	tabakairka.
a pipe,	трубка,	troòbka.
the pelisse,	шуба,	shoòba.

ear-rings, ear-drops, pendants,	серьги,	serghee.
the lace,	кружево,	kroozhaivo.
the umbrella (parasol),	зонтикъ,	zontik.
the stick,	палка, трость,	palka, trost.
a tooth-pick,	зубочистка,	zoobotcheestka.
a ring,	кольцё,	kaltso.
a pin,	булавка,	boolafka.
a needle,	иголка,	eegolka.
scissors,	ножницы,	nozhneetsi.
spectacles,	очки,	atchkeе.
a thimble,	напёрстокъ,	napyorstok.
the thread,	нитка,	neetka.
the cloth,	сукно,	sooknо.
silk,	шёлкъ,	sholk.
money,	деньги,	denghi.
small coin,	мелкія деньги,	mailkya denghi.

Animals.

An eagle,	орёлъ,	aryoll.
an animal,	животное,	zheevotnoyai.
an ass,	осёлъ,	assyoll.
a sheep,	овца,	avtsa.
a cow,	корова,	karova.
an ox,	волъ,	voll.
a bull,	быкъ,	bueek.
a calf,	телёнокъ,	telyonok.
a ram,	баранъ,	baran.
a pig,	свинья,	sveenya.
a horse,	лошадь,	loshed.
a mare,	кобыла,	kabueela.
a dog,	собака,	sabahka.
a cat,	кошка,	koshka.
a cock,	пѣтухъ,	paitookh.
a hen,	курица,	kooritsa.

a chicken,	цыплёнокъ,	tseeplyònok.
a duck,	ýтка,	oòtka.
a goose,	гусь,	gooss.
a turkey,	индюкъ,	eendyoùk.
a turkey-hen,	индюшка,	eendyoùshka.
a pigeon,	гóлубь,	gòloob.
the cattle,	скотъ, скотíпа,	skot, skateèna.
a bear,	медвѣдь,	medvaìd.
a lion,	левъ,	laif.
a hare,	зáяцъ,	zàyaits.
a fox,	лисíца,	leesseètsa.
a spider,	паýкъ,	paoòk.
a mouse,	мышь,	mueesh.
a rat,	крыса,	kreèssa.
a fly,	мýха,	moòkha.
a gnat,	комáръ,	kamàr.
a louse,	вошь,	vosh.
a worm,	червь,	tcherv.
a flea,	блохá,	blakhà.
a bug,	клопъ,	klop.

Writing and study.

The paper,	бумáга,	boomàga.
a pen,	перó,	però.
a steel pen,	стальнóе перó,	stalnòyai però.
the ink,	чернíла,	tcherneèla.
the ink-stand,	чернílница,	tcherneèlitsa.
a letter,	письмó,	peesmò.
wax,	сургýчъ,	soorgoòtch.
a crayon,	карáндашъ,	karandàsh.
a seal,	печáть,	petchàt.
the sand,	песóкъ,	pessòk.
the sand-box,	песóчница,	pessòshnitsa.
a pen-knife,	перочíнный нóжикъ,	perotchìnnee nòzhik.
a rule,	линéйка,	leenèika.

the letters,	бу́квы,	boòkwee.
a bill,	запи́ска,	zapìska.
a book,	кни́га,	kneèga.
a page,	страни́ца,	straneètsa.
a pocket-book,	бума́жникъ,	boomàzhnik.
memorandum-book,	записна́я книжка,	zapisnàya kneèshka.
a quire of paper,	десть,	dest.
a sheet of paper,	листъ бума́ги,	leest boomàghi.
the gazette,	вѣ́домости,	vaìdomosti.
a calendar,	календа́рь,	kalendàr.
a bill, account,	счётъ,	stchott.
study,	уче́ніе,	ootchènyai.
compasses,	ци́ркуль,	tseèrkool.
the language,	язы́къ,	yazeèk.
the word,	сло́во,	slòvo.
painting,	жи́вопись,	zheèvopiss.
science,	нау́ка,	naoòka.
grammar,	грамма́тика,	grammàteeka.
reading,	чте́ніе,	tchtènyai.
writing,	писа́ніе,	pissànyai.
drawing,	рисова́ніе,	rissovànyai.
a draugth,	рису́нокъ,	rissoònok.
ethics,	нравоуче́ніе,	nravaootchènyai.

Man.

The man,	челове́къ,	tchelavèk.
the men (people),	лю́ди,	lyoùdi.
a man,	мущи́на,	moostcheèna.
a woman,	же́нщина,	zhènstcheena.
a child,	дитя́,	deetyà.
a boy,	ма́льчикъ,	màltchik.
a girl,	дѣ́вушка,	daivooshka.
a young man,	ю́ноша, молодо́й челове́къ,	yoùnosha, maladòy tchelavèk.
an old man,	стари́къ,	starik.
an old woman,	стару́ха,	staroòkha.

2

the head,	голова́,	galavà.
the face,	лпцё,	leetsò.
an eye, the eyes,	глазъ, глаза́,	glass, glazàh.
the nose,	носъ,	noss.
the mouth,	ротъ,	roll.
a tooth, the teeth,	зубъ, зу́бы,	zoob, zoobueè.
the lip, the lips,	губа́, гу́бы,	goobàh, goòbuee.
a cheek, the cheeks,	щека́, щёки,	stchèka, stchòkee.
the beard,	борода́,	baradà.
the chin,	подборо́докъ,	podboròdok.
the eye-brows,	бро́вп,	bròvee.
the eye-lids,	вѣки,	vèkee.
the eye-lashes,	рѣснíцы,	resneètsee.
the forehead,	лобъ, чело́,	lop, tshailò.
an ear, the ears,	у́хо, у́шп,	oòkho, oòshee.
the hair,	во́лосы,	vòlossee.
the tongue,	язы́къ,	yazeèk.
the neck,	шéя,	shèya.
the back,	спина́,	speenàh.
a hand, the hands,	рука́, ру́ки,	rookà, roòkee.
a finger, the fingers,	па́лецъ, па́льцы,	pàlets, pàltsee.
the nails,	но́гти,	nòkhtee.
the breast,	грудь,	grood
the stomach,	желу́докъ,	zhailoòdok.
a knee, knees,	колѣно, колѣни,	kalèno, kalènee.
a foot, the feet,	нога́, но́ги,	nagàh, nòghee,
the throat,	го́рло,	gòrlo.
the voice,	го́лосъ,	gòloss.
a bone, the bones,	кость, ко́сти,	kost, kòstee.
the blood,	кровь,	krov.
the pulse,	пульсъ,	pools.
the heart,	сéрдце,	sèrtsai.
the belly,	брю́хо,	bryoùkho.
the soul,	душа́,	dooshàh.
the mind, wit,	умъ, ра́зумъ,	oom, ràzoom.
the thought,	мысль,	mueesl.
the memory,	па́мять,	pàhmet.
the will,	во́ля,	vòlya.

Relationship.

The forefathers,	предки,	prèdkee.
a girl (young lady),	дѣвица,	daiveètsa.
a young lady,	барышня,	bàhreeshnya.
the house-keeper,	хозяинъ, госпо-дінъ,	khazyàheen, gas-padin.
the lord,	баринъ,	bàhrin.
the mistress of the house,	хозяйка, госпожá,	khazyàyka, gas-pazhàh.
a gentlewoman,	барыня,	bàhreenya.
relationship,	родня,	radnyàh.
the father,	отéцъ, батюшка,	atèts, bàtyoushka.
the mother,	мать, матушка,	maht, màhtooshka.
the son,	сынъ,	seen.
the step-son,	пáсынокъ,	pàsseenok.
the son-in-law,	зять,	zyatt,
the daughter,	дочь,	dotch.
the step-daughter,	пáдчерица,	pàhtchaireètsa.
the daughter-in-law,	певéстка,	nevèstka.
the brother,	братъ,	bràht.
the sister,	сестрá, сестрица,	saistrà, saistreètsa.
the uncle,	дядя,	dyàhdya.
the aunt,	тётка,	tyòtka.
the (male) cousin,	двоюродный братъ,	dvayoùrodnee braht.
the (female) cousin,	двоюродная сес-трá,	dvayoùrodnaya saistrà.
the nephew,	племянникъ,	plaimyànnik.
the niece,	племянница,	plaimyànneetsa.
the husband,	мужъ,	moosh.
the wife,	жепà,	zhainà.
a widower,	вдовéцъ,	vdavèts.
a widow,	вдовá,	vdavàh.
a friend,	другъ, пріятель,	drook, preeyàtel.
a (female) friend,	другъ, подрýга,	drook, padroòga.

2*

Natural objects.

The universe,	вселённая,	vsailènnaya.'
the world,	мірь, свѣтъ,	meer, svait.
the (fixed) stars,	свѣтила,	svaiteèla.
the stars,	звѣзды,	zvyòzdee.
the clouds,	облака,	ablakàh.
the air,	воздухъ,	vòzdookh.
the heaven, heavens,	нёбо, небеса,	nèbo, nebessàh.
the sun,	солнце,	sòlntsai.
the moon,	мѣсяцъ, луна,	mèssets, !ooi ʰh.
the earth,	земля,	zaimlyàh.
the water, waters,	вода, воды,	vadàh, vòdee.
the wind,	вѣтръ,	vètr.
the rain,	дождь, дождикъ,	dozhd, dòzhdik.
the fog,	туманъ,	toomàn.
the dust,	пыль,	pueel.
the hail,	градъ,	grad.
the light,	свѣтъ,	svait.
the snow,	снѣгъ,	snaig.
a thunder-storm.	гроза,	grazàh.
the cold,	холодъ,	khòlod.
the frost,	морозъ,	maròss.
the smoke,	дымъ,	deem.
the thaw,	оттепель,	òttaipel.
a rain-bow,	радуга,	ràhdooga.
the heat,	теплота,	taiplotàh.
the thunder,	громъ	grom.
a lightning,	молнія,	mòlnya.
the ice,	лёдъ,	leeott.
the dew,	роса,	rassàh.
a whirlwind,	вихрь,	veekhr.
a forest,	лѣсъ,	laiss.
a meadow,	лугъ,	loog.
a field,	поле,	pòlai.
a ditch, drain,	ровъ,	roﬂ.
a road, way,	дорога,	daròga.
a railway, railroad,	желѣзная дорога,	zhailèznaya daròga.

the locomotive,	паровóзъ,	paravòss.
a path,	дорóжка, тропíнка	daròzhka, trapeènka.
a river,	рѣкá,	raikà.
a tree,	дéрево,	dèrevo.
a flower,	цвѣтóкъ,	tsvaitòk.
the grass,	травá,	travàh.
the oats,	овёсъ,	avyòss.
the hay,	сѣно,	saino.
the straw,	солóма,	salòma.
the corn,	хлѣбъ,	khlaib.
the harvest,	жáтва,	zhàtva.
a mountain,	горá,	garàh.
a pond, pool,	прудъ,	prood.
a rampart,	валъ,	vall.
a cape, head-land,	мысъ,	mweess.
the main land,	твёрдая земля́,	tvyòrdaya zemlyà.
a gulf,	прóливъ,	praliv.
a strait,	залíвъ,	zaliv.
an isthmus,	перешéекъ,	pereshèyek.
the ocean,	океáнъ,	okaiàn.

Time and the principal epochs of the year.

A year,	годъ,	god.
half a year,	пóлгода,	pòlgoda.
the month,	мѣсяцъ,	mèssets.
three months.	три мѣсяца,	tree mèssetsa.
six months,	шесть мѣсяцевъ,	shest mèssetsef.
a week,	недѣля,	nedàilya.
fortnight,	двѣ недѣли,	dvai nedàilee.
the day,	день,	den.
the evening,	вéчеръ,	vètchair.
the night,	ночь,	notch.
the morning,	ýтро,	oòtro.
noon,	пóлдень,	pòlden.
midnight,	пóлночь,	pòlnotch.

the hour,	часъ,	tchass.
half an hour,	пóлчаса,	pòltchassa.
quarter of an hour,	чéтверть часà,	tchètvert tchassàh.
the time,	врéмя,	vrèmya.
date (of the month),	числó,	tcheeslò.
the birth day,	рождéнье,	rozhdènyai.
Saint's day,	имявúны,	eemaineèni.
Saint's day (of a prince),	тезоименúтство,	taizoeemaineètstvo.
the spring,	веснà,	vaisnà.
the summer,	лѣто,	lèto.
the autumn,	óсень,	òssen.
the winter,	зимà,	zeemàh.
sunday,	воскресéнье,	vaskraissènyai.
monday,	понедѣльникъ,	panaidèlnik.
twesday,	втóрникъ,	ftòrnik.
wednesday,	середà,	seredà.
thursday,	четвертóкъ,	tchetvertòk.
friday,	пятница,	pyàtneetsa.
saturday,	суббóта,	soòbbota.
the new year,	нóвый годъ,	nòwee god.
Christmas,	Рождествó Христóво,	razhdaistvò khreestòvo.
the Twelfth-day,	Крещéніе,	kraistchènyai.
the carnival,	мáсляница,	màslaineetsa.
the lent,	велúкій постъ,	vaileèkee post.
Easter,	Пáсха, Свѣтлое Воскресéніе,	pàskha, svètloyai voskraissènyai.
Ascension Sunday,	Вознесéніе,	voznaissènyai.
Whitsuntide,	Дýховъ День,	doòkhof den.
Trinity Sunday,	Трóпцынъ день,	tròeetsin den.
Assumption,	Успéніе,	oospènyai.
mid-summer's day,	Ивáновь день,	eevànof den.
January,	январь,	yanvàr.
February,	феврáль,	faivràl.
March,	мартъ,	mart.
April,	апрѣль,	aprèl.
May,	май,	mey.

June,	iюнь,	youn.
July,	iюль,	youl.
August,	áвгустъ,	àvgoost.
September,	сентябрь,	sentyàbr.
October,	октябрь,	actyàbr.
November,	ноябрь,	nayàbr.
December,	декабрь,	dekàbr.
to-day,	сегóдня,	saivòdnee.
yesterday,	вчерá,	ftchairàh.
the day before yester-day,	трéтьяго дня,	trètyava dnee.
to-morrow,	зáвтра,	zàftra.
after to-morrow,	пóслѣ зáвтра,	pòslai zaftra.
afternoon,	пóслѣ обѣда,	pòslai abèda.
this morning,	сегóдня по утрý,	saivòdnee pa ootroò.
to-morrow evening,	зáвтра вéчеромъ,	zàftra vètcherom.

Countries and nations.

Russia,	Россія,	rasseèa.
a Russian,	россіянинъ, рýс-скій,	rasseéyanin, roòs-kee.
France,	Фрáнція,	fràntzya.
a Frenchman,	французъ,	frantsoòz.
England,	Áнглія,	ànglya.
an Englishman,	англичáнинъ,	angleetchànin.
Spain,	Испáнія,	eespànya.
a Spaniard,	испáнецъ,	eespànets.
Italy,	Итáлія,	eetàlya.
an Italian,	италіянецъ,	eetalyànets.
Germany,	Гермáнія,	ghermànya.
a German,	нѣмецъ,	naìmets.
Austria,	Áвстрія,	àvstrya.
an Autsrian,	австріецъ,	avstreèyets.
Prussia,	Прýссія,	proòssya.
a Prussian,	прусáкъ,	proossàk.
Holland,	Голлáндія,	gollàndya.
a Dutchman,	голлáндецъ,	gollàndets.

Sweden,	Швеція,	shevètsya.
a Swede,	шведъ,	shvaid.
Danemark,	Данія,	dàhnya.
a Dane,	датчанинъ, .	dàhtchanin.
Switzerland,	Швейцарія,	shveitsàhrya.
a Swiss,	швейцарецъ,	shveitsàrets.
Poland,	Польша,	pòlsha.
a Pole,	полякъ,	palyàk.
Portugal,	Португалія,	partoogàlia.
a Portuguese,	португалецъ,	partoogàlets.
Turkey,	Турція,	toòrtsia.
a Turc,	турокъ,	toòrok.
Hungary,	Венгрія,	vaìngria.
a Hungarian,	венгерецъ,	vainghèrets.
Greece,	Греція,	grètsia.
a Greek,	грекъ,	graik.
Asia,	Азія,	àhzia.
an Asiatic,	азіятецъ,	aziàhtets.
Africa,	Африка,	àfreeka.
an Afrikan,	африканецъ,	afreekànets.
America,	Америка,	amèreeka.
an American,	американецъ,	amereekànets.
Oceania,	Австралія,	avstràhlia.
Egypt,	Египетъ,	yegheèpet.
an Egyptian,	египтянинъ,	yegheèptianin.
Persia,	Персія,	pèrsia.
a Persian,	персіянинъ,	perseeyànin.
a Jew,	жидъ, еврей,	zheed, yevrèi.
the Indias,	Индія,	eèndia.
an Indian,	индѣецъ,	eendàiyets.
China,	Китай,	keetày.
a Chinese,	китаецъ,	keetàhyets.
Japan,	Японія,	yapònia.
a Japanese,	японецъ,	yapònets.
a state,	государство,	gassoodàrstvo.
an empire,	имперія,	impaìria.
a kingdom,	королевство,	karalaìvstvo.
a republic,	республика,	respoòblika.

Numbers.

one,	одйнъ, *f.* однá,	ahdin, ahdnà.
two,	два, *f.* двѣ,	dva, dvai.
three,	три,	tree.
four,	четы́ре,	tcheteėrai.
five,	пять,	pait.
six,	шесть,	shaist.
seven,	семь,	saim.
eight,	вóсемь,	vòssaim.
nine,	дéвятъ,	daìvet.
ten,	дéсять,	daisset.
eleven,	одйпнадцать,	ahdinnatset.
twelve,	двѣнáдцать,	dvainàtset.
thirteen,	трипáдцать,	treenàtset.
fourteen,	четы́рнадцать,	tchetcérnatset.
fifteen,	пятнáдцать,	paitnàtset.
sixteen,	шестнáдцать,	shaistnàtset.
seventeen,	семнáдцать,	saimnàtset.
eigtheen,	осьмнáдцать, во-	asmnàtset, vossaim-
	семпáдцать,	nàtset.
nineteen,	девятнáдцать,	daivetnàtset.
twenty,	двáдцать,	dvàtset.
twenty one, etc.	двáдцать одйнъ,	dvàstet ahdìn.
thirty,	трйдцать,	treètset.
forty,	сóрокъ,	sòrok.
fifty,	пятьдесятъ,	paitdessiàt.
sixty,	шестьдесятъ,	shaistdessiàt.
seventy,	сéмдесятъ,	saìmdesset.
eigthy,	вóсемьдесятъ,	vòssaimdesset.
ninety,	девянóсто,	daivenòsto.
hundred,	сто,	sto.
two hundred,	двѣ́сти,	dvaìstee.
three hundred,	трйста,	treèsta.
four hundred,	четы́реста,	tcheteèresta.
five hundred,	пятьсóтъ,	paitsòt.
six hundred,	шестьсóтъ,	chaistsòt.

a thousand,	тысяча,	teèssetcha.
two thousand, etc.	двѣ тысячи,	dvai teèssetchee.
five thousand, etc.	пять тысячъ,	pait teèssetch.
a million,	миллióнъ,	milleeòn.
*	*	*
the first,	пéрвый,	pèrwec.
the second,	вторóй, другóй,	ftaròy, droogòy.
the third,	трéтiй,	traìtee.
the fourth,	четвёртый,	tchetvyòrtee.
the-fifth,	пятый,	paìtee.
the sixth,	шестóй,	shaistòy.
the seventh,	седьмóй,	saidmòy.
the eighth,	осьмóй,	asmòi.
the ninth,	девятый,	devyàtee.
the tenth,	десятый,	dessyàtee,
the eleventh,	одиннадцатый,	adeènnatsatee.
the twelfth,	двѣнáдцатый,	dvainàtsatee, (ftaròy
	(вторóй нáдесять),	nàdesset).
the twentieth,	двадцáтый,	dvatsàtee.
the twenty first, etc.	двáдцать пéрвый,	dvàtset pèrwee.
the thirtieth,	тридцáтый,	treetsàtee.
the fortieth,	сороковóй,	sarakavòy.
the fiftieth, etc	пятидесятый,	paiteedessyàtee.
the hundredth,	сóтый,	sòtee.
hundredth and first,	сто пéрвый,	sto pèrwee.
the thousandth,	тысящный,	teèssyashtnee.
the millionth,	миллióнный,	milliònnee.
*	*	*
the half,	половина,	palaveèna.
the third part,	треть,	trait.
the quart,	чéтверть,	tchètvert.
one and a half,	полторá,	paltaràh.
the double,	вдвóе,	vdvòyai.
the triple,	втрóе,	ftròyai.
ten, half a score,	десятокъ,	dessyàtok.
a dozen,	дюжина,	dyoòzheena.
a hundred,	сóтня,	sòtnya.

PRONOUNS.

NOMINATIVE.	GENIT. and ACCUS.	DATIVE.	INSTRUMENTAL.
I,	of me; me,	to me,	by me,
я, *ya.*	меня, *menyà.*	мнѣ, *mnyai.*	мнóю,*mnòyou.*
thou,	of thee; thee,	to thee,	by thee,
ты, *tee.*	тебя, *tebyà.*	тебѣ, *taibai.*	тобóю,*tabòyou*
he,	of him; him,	to him,	by him,
онъ, *onn.*	егó, *yaivò.*	емý, *yaimoò.*	имъ, *yeem.*
she,	of her; her,	to her,	by her,
анá, *anà.*	ея, её, *yaiyò.*	ей, *yèy.*	éю, *yaìyou.*
we,	of us; us,	to us,	by us,
мы, *mwee.*	насъ, *nass.*	намъ, *nam.*	нáми, *nàmee.*
you,	of you; you,	to you,	by you,
вы, *wee.*	васъ, *vass.*	вамъ, *vam.*	вáми, *vàmee.*
they,	of them; them,	the them,	by them,
онú, *aneè.*	ихъ, *yeekh.*	имъ, *yeem.*	úми, *yeèmee.*
they,	of them; them,	to them,	by them,
онѣ, *anai.*	ихъ, *yeekh.*	имъ, *yeem.*	úми, *yeèmee.*
—	of himself,	to himself,	by himself,
—	себя, *saibyà.*	себѣ, *saibai.*	собóю,*sabòyou*
who, which?	whose; whom?	to whom?	by whom?
кто, *khto.*	когó, *kavò.*	комý, *kamoò.*	къмъ, *kaim.*
what?	of which; what?	to what?	by what,
что, *shto.*	чегó, *tshaivò.*	чемý, *tshaimoò.*	чѣмъ, *tshaim.*

MASCULINE.	FEMININE.	NEUTER.
My, mine,	my, mine,	
мой, *moy.*	моя, *mayà.*	моё, *mayò.*
thy, thine,	thy, thine,	
твой, *tvoy.*	твоя, *tvayà.*	твоé, *tvayò.*
his,	hers,	
егó, свой, *yevò,svoy.*	ея, своя, *yeiò, svayà.*	соё, *svayò.*
ours,	ours,	
нашъ, *nash.*	нáша, *nàsha.*	нáше, *nàshai.*

MASCULINE.	FEMININE.	NEUTER.
yours,	yours,	вáше, *vàshay.*
вашъ, *vash.*	вáша, *vàsha.*	
theirs,	theirs,	
ихъ, *yeekh.*	ихъ, *yeekh.*	} *for the three genders.*
ours,	yours,	
нáши, *nàshee.*	вáши, *vàshee.*	
what?	what?	
котóрый, *katòree.*	котóрая, *katòraya.*	котóрое, *katòroyai.*
this, сей, *sey,*	this, сiя, *seeyà.*	this, cié, *seeyaì*
that, тотъ, *tott.*	that, та, *ta.*	that, то, *to.*
whose? чей, *tshey.*	чья, *tshya.*	чьё, *tshyo.*

PREPOSITIONS.

In, to,	въ, во,	v', vo.
on, upon, to,	на,	na.
with,	съ, со,	s', so.
after, near,	по,	po.
at, by,	у,	oo.
without,	безъ,	baiz.
till, to,	до,	do.
of, from,	отъ,	ott.
for, by, against,	за, для,	za, dleea.
before, for,	прéжде, предъ,	prèzhdai, praid.
from, between,	изъ,	eez.
after, behind,	пóслѣ, позадú,	pòslai, pazadee.
beside, near,	пóдлѣ,	pòdlai.
to, towards,	къ, ко,	k', ko.
upon over,	надъ,	nad.
under,	подъ,	pod.
of, round, against,	о, объ, обо,	o, ob, obo.
from behind,	изъ-зá,	eez-za.
from under,	изъ-пóдъ,	eez-pod.

29

CONJUNCTIONS.

And,	и, а.	ee, a.
as, when,	какъ,	kak.
because,	и́бо,	eèbo.
thus, so,	такъ,	tàk.
but,	одна́ко,	adnàko.
when, whenever,	когда́,	kaghdà.
but,	но,	no.
but, however,	одна́ко жъ,	adnàkozh.
because,	потому́ что,	patamoò shto.
or, otherwise,	и́ли, ли́бо,	eèle, leèbo.
if, in case, when,	е́жели, е́сли,	yàizhelee, yèslee.
therefore,	по сему́,	pa saimoò.
though, although,	хотя́,	khatyà.
that, in order that,	что, чтобы́, чтобъ,	shto, shtobwee, shtob.
if, whether.	ли.	lee.

ADVERBS.

Yes, so,	да, такъ,	da, tak.
no, not,	нѣтъ,	nyaitt.
no,	пе,	nyai.
nothing,	ничего́,	neetchaivò.
much,	мно́го,	mnògo.
little,	ма́ло,	màlo.
very, greatly,	о́чень, весьма́,	òtchen, vaismà.
almost,	почти́,	patshtee.
enough,	дово́льно,	davòlno.
only,	то́лько,	tòlko.
quickly, fast,	ско́ро,	skòro.
faster,	поскорѣе,	paskaraìyai.
gently, softly,	ти́хо, потихо́ньку,	teèkho,pateekhònkoo
more gently,	ти́ше,	teéshai.
where, whither,	гдѣ, куда́,	gdyai, koodà.
here, hither,	здѣсь, сюда́,	zdyess, soodà.
there, thither,	тамъ, туда́,	tam, toodà.

somewhere,	гдѣ нибудь,	ghdyaì nibood.
eyrerywhere,	вездѣ,	vezdaì.
bad, badly,	хýдо, дýрно,	khoòdo, doòrno.
good, well,	хорошó, добрó,	kharashò, dabrò.
why, how?	для чегó? почемý? за чѣмъ?	dleea tshevò? patshémoò? zatchèm?
why not?	по чемý нѣтъ?	pa tshémoò nyaitt?
always,	всегдá,	fsaigdà.
how much?	скóлько?	skòlko.
as much as,	стóлько,	stòlko.
often,	чáсто,	tchàsto.
seldom,	рѣдко,	raìdko.
sometimes,	иногдá,	eenagdà.
ugly,	мéрзко,	maìrzko.
warmly,	теплó,	taiplò.
coldly,	хóлодно,	khòlodno.
gayly, lively,	вéсело,	vaìsselo.
sorrowfully,	печáльно,	paitchàlno.
greatly,	велúко,	vaileèko.
little,	мáло,	màlo.
dryly,	сýхо,	soòkho.
wet, moist,	мóкро,	mòkro.
a long time,	дóлго,	dòlgo.
long ago,	давнó,	davnò.
purposely,	парóчно,	naròshno.
in vain,	напрáсно,	napràsno.
soon,	скóро,	skòro.
afterwards,	пóслѣ, потóмъ,	pòslai, patòm.
immediately,	тóтчасъ, сей часъ,	tòttchass, sey tchass.
dearly, dear,	дóрого,	dòrogo.
cheaply, cheap,	дёшево,	deeòshevo,
by little and little,	по-малéньку,	pa malènkoo.
when?	когдá?	kaghdà.
truly, indeed,	прáвда,	pràdva.
certainly,	конéчно,	kanèshno.
nowhere,	нигдѣ,	neegdyaì.
at present, actually,	тепéрь, нынѣ,	taipèr, neènay.

never,	никогда́,	neekagdà.
then, at that time,	тогда́,	tagdà.
hence forth,	впредь,	fpraid.
almost, nearly,	чуть,	tchoot.
already,	уже́,	oozhai.
late,	по́здно,	pòzdo.
early,	ра́но,	ràno.
thus, so,	такъ,	tak.
yet,	еще́,	yeshetchò.
not yet,	нѣтъ еще́,	nyell yeshtchò.

OBSERVATION. The words *is, are* (in the present tense of the indicative of the auxiliary verb *to be*), being generally understood in the Russian language, the great attention must be paid to the adverbs underneath, since they constitute an essential part of speech; ex. здѣсь, *zdyess*, as an adverb, means only *here*. Thus the usual answer to the question: *is he here?* здѣсь ли онъ? *zdyess li onn?* is: онъ здѣсь, *onn zdiess* (he here), or simply, здѣсь, *zdyess*, which means *he is* (they are) *here*. Several other adverbs are in the same case, as: *it is true*, пра́вда, *pràvdah; that is well*, хорошо́, *hharashò; it is not necessary*, не на́добно, *nyai nàdobno; it is cold*, хо́лодно, *khòlodno*, etc. But the verb *to be* is only suppressed in the present tense; in the preterit one says: *he was here*, онъ былъ здѣсь, *onn bweel zdess*, and in the future: *he will be here*, онъ бу́детъ здѣсь, *onn boòdett zdess*.

ADJECTIVES.

Great,	вели́кій, большо́й,	veleèkee, balshòy.
little,	ма́лый,	màhlee.
bad,	худо́й, дурно́й,	khoodòy, doornòy.
grateful,	благода́рный,	blagodàhrnee.
polite,	учти́вый,	ootchteèwee.
unmannerly,	гру́бый,	groòbwee.

old,	ста́рый,	stàrhee.
young,	молодо́й,	maladòy.
new,	но́вый,	nòwee.
beautiful,	краси́вый,	krasseèwee.
ugly,	дурно́й,	doornòy,
deformed,	безобра́зный,	baizobràznee.
wise, (prudent),	му́дрый, у́мный,	moòdree, oòmnee.
stupid,	глу́пый,	gloòpwee.
free, (independent),	во́льный, свобо́д-ный,	vòlnee, svabòdnee.
happy,	счастли́вый,	stchastleèwee.
unhappy,	несча́стный,	nestchàsnee.
gracious,	ми́лостивый,	meèlosteewee.
affable,	ла́сковый,	làskowee.
amiable,	любе́зный, ми́лый,	lyoubèznee, meèlee.
white,	бѣ́лый,	baìlee.
black,	чёрный,	tchòrnee.
red,	кра́сный,	kràsnee.
green,	зелёный,	zailyònee.
blue,	голубо́й,	galooboy.
deep blue,	си́ній,	seènee.
yellow,	жёлтый,	zhòltee.
gray,	сѣ́рый,	saìree.
rosy-coloured,	ро́зовый,	ròzowee.
of silver,	сере́бряный,	seraìbrenee.
of gold,	золото́й,	zalatòy.
of stone,	ка́менный,	kàmennee.
of wood,	деревя́нный,	derevyànnee.
of iron,	желѣ́зный,	zhelaìznee.
of steel,	стально́й,	stalnòy.
of copper,	мѣ́дный,	maìdnee.

*

*   *

OBSERVATION. The feminine gender of adjectives is formed by changing the final syllable into ая, *aya*, and the
neuter by changing the final syllable into ое, *oyai*. Ex.

MASCULINE.	FEMININE.	NEUTER.
The great captain, велйкій полково-децъ, vaileékee palkavò-dets.	the grand-duchess, велйкая княгйня, vaileèkaya knya-gheènya:	the great exploit, велйкое дѣло, vaileèkoyai dailo.

The comparative degree of adjectives is formed by changing the syllable of the positive into *ѣe* for the comparative, and into *ѣйшій* for the superlative, or by adding for the superlative the words сáмый, *sàhmwe*, or пре, *prai*, joined before the positive; ex.

POSITIVE.	COMPARATIVE.	SUPERLATIVE.
Good, дóбрый, dò-bree,	добрѣе, dabraìyai,	добрѣ́йшій, dabréy-tshee, or сáмый дóбрый, sàhmwee dòbree.
famous, слáвный, slàvnee,	славнѣе, slavnaìyai,	славнѣ́йшій, slav-nèyshee, or пре-слáвный, préslàv-nee.

The following adjectives are irregular :

стрóгій,	stròghee,	severe.
дорогóй,	daragòy,	dear.
лёгкій,	lyòkhkee,	light.
молодóй,	maladòy,	young.
ýзкій,	oòzkee,	narrow.
велйкій, большóй,	vaileèkee, balshòy,	great.
мáлый,	màhlee,	little.
дóбрый, хорóшій,	dòbree, kharòshee,	good.
высóкій,	weesòkee,	high.
	COMPARATIVE.	
стрóже,	stròzhai,	more severe,
дорóже,	daròzhai,	dearer,
лéгче,	laìkhtchai,	lighter,
молóже,	malòzhai,	younger,
ýже,	oòzhai,	narrower.

3

бо́льше,	bòlshai,	greater.
ме́ньше,	maìnshai,	less.
лу́чше,	loòtchai,	better.
вы́ше,	weèshai,	higher.

SUPERLATIVE.

строжа́йшій,	strozhàyshee,	the most severe.
дража́йшій,	drazhàyshee,	the dearest.
легча́йшій,	laikhtchàyshee,	the lightest.
мла́дшій,	mlàdshee,	the youngest.
бо́льшій,	bòlshee,	the greatest.
ме́ньшій,	maìnshee,	the least.
лу́чшій,	loòtchee,	the better.
высоча́йшій,	weesotchàyshee,	the highest.

OBSERVATION. In the Russian language a particular termination serves to express a small degree or excess of a quality in certain adjectives; as: зелёный, zailyònee, *green*, is changed into зеленёшенекъ, zailainyòshenek, *entirelye green*, and зеленова́тый, zailainavàtee, *greenish;* of сыро́й, seeròy, *raw*, is formed сырова́тый, seeravàtee, *a little raw*, etc.

VERBS.

All the forms of the tenses, in the conjugation of Russian verbs, are regulated on the infinitive. The regular verbs are invariably terminated in атъ, ятъ, ѣтъ, итъ, отъ, утъ; the most part of irregular verbs are monosyllabic, or are terminated in зтъ, стъ, чь or тп.

The personal pronouns я, *ya*, I; ты, *tee*, thou; онъ, *onn*, he; она́, *anàh*, she; мы, *mwee*, we; вы, *wee*, you; они́, *aneè;* онѣ, *anaì*, *they*, are often suppressed in the present of the indicative; thus one may say: зна́ю, *znàhyou*, I know, in place of я зна́ю, *ya znàhyou*.

The present of the indicative of verbs is conjugated as follows:

FIRST FORM.

Those which have ешь in the second person:

I give,	я даю́,	ya dayoù.
thou givest,	ты даёшь,	tee dayòsh.
he, she gives,	онъ, она́ даётъ,	onn, anàh dayòtt.
we give,	мы даёмъ,	mwe dayòm.
you give,	вы даёте,	wee dayòtai.
they give,	они́, онѣ даю́тъ,	aneé, anai dayoùt.

SECOND FORM.

Those which have ишь in the second person:

I speak,	я говорю́,	ya gavaroò.
thou speakest,	ты говори́шь,	tee gavareèsh.
he, she speaks,	онъ, она́ говори́тъ,	onn, anàh gavareèt.
we speak,	мы говори́мъ,	mwe gavareèm.
you speak,	вы говори́те,	wee gavareètai.
they speak,	они́, онѣ говоря́тъ,	aneè anai gavaràht.

The past tense, whose conjugation is given underneath, corresponds to the imperfect, perfect and pluperfect tenses in the conjugation of English verbs. Generally the verbs whose infinitive ends in ть with a vowel, change for the past tense ть into лъ for the masculine, ла for the feminine, and ло for the neuter. The three persons of the plural never vary, whatever may be the gender of the subject, and end always in ли.

PAST TENSE,

I have given,	я далъ, *fem.* дала́,	ya dahl *or* dalàh.
thou hast given,	ты далъ, *or* дала́,	tee dahl *or* dalàh,
he, she has given,	онъ далъ, она́ дала́,	onn dahl, anà dalàh.
	neut. оно́ да́ло,	anó dàhlo.
we have given,	мы да́ли,	mwe dàhlee.
you have given,	вы да́ли,	wee dàhlee.
they have given,	они́, онѣ да́ли,	aneè, anai dàhlee.

3*

PAST TEMSe.

I have spoken,	я говори́лъ, *fem.* гряори́ла,	ya gavareèl *or* gavareèla.
thou hast spoken,	ты говори́лъ *or* говори́ла,	tee gavareèl *or* gavareèla.
he, she has spoken,	онъ говори́лъ, она́ говори́ла, *neut.* оно́ говори́ло,	on gavareel, anà gavareèla, anò gavareèle.
we have spoken,	мы говори́ли,	mwe gavareèlee,
you have spoken,	вы говори́ли,	wee gavareèlee,
they have spoken,	они́, онѣ говори́ли,	aneè,anaigavareèlee,

The future tense, in certain verbs, has a simple form; but is most generally formed with the future of the auxiliary verb бытъ, *bweet, to be,* wich is conjugated with the infinitive of the principal verb.

SIMPLE FUTURE.

I shall give,	я дамъ,	ya dam.
thou wilt give,	ты дашь,	tee dash.
he, she will give,	онъ, она́ дастъ,	onn, anà dast.
we shall give,	мы дади́мъ,	mwe dadeèm.
you will give,	вы дади́те,	wee dedeètai.
they will give,	они́, онѣ даду́тъ,	aneè, anai dadoòt.

COMPOUND FUTURF.

I shall speak,	я бу́ду говори́ть,	ya boòdoo gavareèt.
thou wilt speak,	ты бу́дешь говори́ть,	tee boòdesh gavareèt.
he, she will speak,	онъ, она́ бу́детъ говори́ть,	onn, anà boòdet gavareèt.
we shall speak,	мы бу́демъ говори́ть,	mwe boòdem gavareèt.
you will speak,	вы бу́дете говори́ть,	wee boòdaite gavareèt.
they will speak,	они́, онѣ бу́дутъ говори́ть,	aneè, anai boòdoot gavareèt.

As almost all the simple future tenses are conjugated regularly as the present tense, the three principal tenses, the present, perfect and future, offer no serious difficulty.

The conditional and subjonctive moods are not to be found in the conjugation of Russian verbs. The conditional form is expressed by the preterit, joined to the particle бы, bwe; ex. я бы писáлъ, ya bwe peessàll, *I should write.* The subjunctive is designated in the Russian language by the conjunction чтобы before a consonant, or чтобъ before a vowel; ex. *I wish that he may write,* я желáю чтобъ опъ писáлъ, ya zhailàyou shtob onn pessàll.

The imperative mood is generally formed of the present of the indicative in the following manner: я знáю, ya znàyou, *I know;* imper. знай, znày, *know;* я пишý, ya peeshoó, *I write;* imper. пиши, peesheè, *write.* The plural is formed by adding the syllable те: знáйте, znàytai, *know you;* пишите, peesheètai, *write you.*

In place of the English indefinite pronoun *one,* the Russians make use of the third plural person of the verb; ex. *one says,* говорятъ, gavaràht (they, say, people *or* persons say).

The interrogative form is expressed in the Russian language by placing the particle ли beetween the verb and the subject whether noun or pronoun. Ex. *do you speak the Russian language?* говорите ли вы цо-рýсски? gavareètai le wee pa-roòskee?

The negative particle не, nai, is placed between the subject and the verb: *I do not wish,* я не хочý, ya nai khatchoò; *the master does not wish,* учитель не хóчетъ, ootcheètel nai khòtchet; *dost thou not know?* не знáешь ли ты? nai znàyesh lee tee?

In place of the affirmative párticle да, da, *yes;* такъ, tak, *thus,* the Russians often employ the principal verb in the sentence or a word which indicates that the verb is understood.

John, is the tailor here?	Ивáнъ, здѣсь ли портнóй?	Eevàn! zdyes lee partnòy?
yes, sir,	здѣсь, сýдарь,	zdyes, soòdar, (that is: here, sir; he is here).
Is he come here?	Былъ ли онъ здѣсь?	bweel lee on zdyes?
yes, Madam,	былъ, судáрыня,	bweel, soodàreenya, (that is: he was, he is come, Madam).
Have you paper (to sell)?	Есть ли у васъ бумáги?	yest lee oo vas boomàhghi?

that is to say: is to you any paper?

| yes, sir, | есть, сýдарь, | yest (here is), soòdar. |

OBSERVATION. In familiar conversation one frequently hears the words да'съ, da'ss, *yes, sir;* чегó'съ, tchaivò'ss? *what, Madam?* in place of да, Садýрь, *da, soòdar;* чегó, Судáрыня? *tchaivò,* soodàhrynia

CONJUGATION OF SOME VERBS ACCORDING TO THE TWO PRECEDING FORMS.

The verbs noted I are conjugated after the first form, and those noted II according to the second.

I.

To have,	имѣть,	eemàit.
I have,	я имѣю,	ya eemaìyou.
I had, have had,	я имѣлъ,	ya eemaìl.
I shall have,	я бýду имѣть,	ya boòdoo eemaìt.

to know,	знать,	znate.
I know,	я знаю,	ya znàyou.
I knew, have known,	я зналъ,	ya znall.
I shall know,	я буду знать,	ya boòdoo znat.

to read,	читать,	tcheetàt.
I read,	я читаю,	ya tcheetàyou.
I read, have read,	я чпталъ,	ya tcheetàll.
I shall read,	я буду читать,	ya boòdoo tcheetàt.

to write,	ппсать,	peessàt.
I write,	я пишу,	ya peeshoò.
I wrote, have written,	я ппсалъ,	ya peessàll.
I shall write,	я буду ппсать,	ya boòdoo pcessàt.

to be,	быть,	bweet.
I am,	я (есмь, *suppressed*),	ya (yesm).
I was, have been,	я былъ,	ya bweel.
I shall be,	я буду,	ya boòdoo.

to show,	показывать, показать,	pakàzeevat, pakazàt.
I show,	я показываю,	ya pakàzeevayou.
I showed,	я показывалъ,	ya pakàzeevall.
I have shown,	я показалъ,	ya pakazàll.
I shall show, *or*	я буду показывать, *or*	ya boòdoo pakàzee-vat.
I will show,	я покажу,	ya pakazhoò.

to send,	посылать, послать,	passeelàt, paslàt.
I send,	я посылаю,	ya passeelàyou.
I sent,	я посылалъ,	ya passeelàll.
I have sent,	я послалъ,	ya paslàll.
I shall *or* will send,	я буду посылать	ya boòdoo passeelàt.
	я пошлю,	ya pashlyoù.

And also the following verbs:

to wish,	желáть,	zhailàt.
I wish,	я желáю,	ya zhailàyou.
to do, to make,	дѣлать, сдѣлать,	dyailal, zdyailat.
to take a walk,	гулять,	goolyàt.
to print,	печáтать,	paitchàtat.
to traffic,	торговáть,	targovàt.
I traffic,	я торгýю,	ya targoòyou.
to kiss,	цѣловáть,	tsailavàt.
to draw,	рисовáть,	reessovàt.
to possess, I possess,	владѣть, я владѣю,	vladait, ya vladaiyou.
to have pity,	жалѣть,	zhailèt.
to drink, I drink,	пить, я пью,	peet, ya peeyou.
to move,	двигать, двинуть,	dveègat, dveènoot.
I move,	я двигаю,	ya dveègayou.
I shall move,	я двину,	ya dveènoo.
to say,	скáзывать,сказáть,	zkàzeevat, skazàt.
I say	я скáзываю,	ya skàzeevayou.
I shall say,	я скажý,	ya skazhoò.
to forget,	забывáть, забыть,	zabweevàt, zabweèt.
to perish,	погибáть, погиб-нуть,	pagheebàt, pagheèb-noot,
to buy,	покупáть, купить,	pakoopàt, koopeèt,

II.

To pray,	просить,	prasseèt.
I pray,	я прошý,	ya prashoò.
I prayed, have prayed,	я просилъ,	ya prasseèl.
I shall pray,	я бýду просить,	ya boòdoo prasseèt.

to accuse,	винить,	veeneèt.
I accuse,	я виню,	ya veenyoù.
I accused, have accused,	я винилъ,	ya veeneèl.
I shall accuse,	я бýду винить,	ya boòdoo veeneèt.

to look,	смотрѣть,	smatrèt.
I look,	я смотрю́,	ya smatroò.
I looked, have looked,	я смотрѣлъ,	ya smatrèll.
I shall look,	я бу́ду смотрѣть,	ya boòdoo smatrèt.

to fear,	бояться,	bahyàtsa.
I fear,	я бою́сь,	ya bahyoùss.
I feared, have feared,	я боя́лся,	ya bahyàlsa.
I shall fear,	я бу́ду бояться,	ya boòdoo bahyàtsa.

to love,	люби́ть,	lewbeèt.
I love,	я люблю́,	ya lewblèw.
I loved, have loved,	я люби́лъ,	ya lewbeèll.
I shall *or* will love,	я бу́ду люби́ть,	ya boòdoo lewbeét.

to nourish,	корми́ть,	karmeèt.
I nourish,	я кормлю́	ya karmlèw.
I nourished, have nourished,	я корми́лъ,	ya karmeèl.
I shall nourish,	я бу́ду корми́ть,	ya boòdoo karmeèt.

to come,	приходи́ть, придти́,	preekhadeèt, preetteè.
I come,	я прихожу́,	ya preekhazhoò.
I came,	я приходи́лъ,	ya preekhadeèll.
I have come,	я пришёлъ,	ya preeshòll.
I will *or* shall come,	я бу́ду приходи́ть, *or*	ya boòdoo preekhadeèt.
	я приду́,	ya preedoò.

to bring,	приноси́ть, принести́,	preenosseèt, preenaisteè.
I bring,	я принишу́,	ya preenashoò.
I brought,	я приноси́лъ,	ya preenasseèl.
I have brought,	я принёсъ,	ya preenyòss.
I shall *or* will bring,	я бу́ду приноси́ть, *or*	ya boòdoo preenasseèt.
	я принесу́,	ya preenessoò.

And also the following verbs:

to believe,	вѣрить,	vaireet.
I believe,	я вѣрю,	ya vairoo.
to boil,	варить,	vareèt.
to order,	велѣть,	vailèt.
to stand,	стоять,	stahyàt.
I stand,	я стою,	ya stahyoù.
to heat, I heat,	топить, я топлю,	tapeèt, ya taplèw.
to suffer, (I suffer),	терпѣть, (я тер-плю),	terpèt, (ya terplèw).
to see, (I see),	видѣть, (я вижу),	veedèt, (ya veézhoo).
to extinguish,	гасить, (я гашу),	gasseèt, (ya gashoò).
to flatter,	льстить, (я льщу),	lsteet, (yal'shtchoo).
to avenge,	мстить, (я мщу),	msteet, (ya m'shtchoo).
to drive,	гнать, (я гоню),	gnaht,(ya gan-yoù).
to sleep,	спать, (я сплю),	spaht, (va spl-yoù).
to will, I will,	хотѣть, я хочу,	khatèt. ya khatchoò.
I shall wish,	я захочу,	ya zakhatchoò.
to conduct,	проводить, про-вести,	pravadeèt,pravesteè.
I conduct,	я провожу,	ya pravazhoò.
I shall conduct,	я проведу,	ya pravaidoò.

OBSERVATION. We see from what precedes that the conjugation of Russian verbs, in the three principal tenses, offers no difficulty. We need only remark the final syllables in the present tense, as it is in conformity with them that all the other tenses are conjugated.

DIALOGUES.

DIALOGUE I.

Good morning, Sir,	Здра́вствуйте, Госуда́рь мой (Су́дарь),	zdràstweete gossoodàr moy (soòdar),
Good evening, Madam, (Ma'am, Miss),	Здра́вствуйте, Суда́рыня,	zdràstweete,soodàhreenya.
Good morning (evening), my dear,	Здра́вствуй, другъ мой! (бра́тъ!)	zdràstwee, drook moy (braht)!
Welcome!	Добро́ пожа́ловать!	dabrò pazhàlovat!
Walk in!	Войди́те!	voydeète!
Come up!	Взойди́те!	vzoydeète!
Pray be seated where you please,	Сади́тесь, гдѣ вамъ уго́дно,	sadeètéss gdai vam oogòdno.
How have you rested?	Какъ вы почива́ли?	kak wee patcheevàleè?
How are you?	Какъ вы поживаете?	kak wee pazheevayaite?
Tolerably,	Изря́дно,	eezreeàdno.
How is your health?	Каково́ ва́ше здоро́вье?	kakavò vàshe zdaròvyai?
Are you in good health?	Здоро́вы ли вы?	zdaròwee lee wee?
Art thou in good health?	Здоро́въ ли ты?	zdaròf lee tee?
Perfectly well, thank God!	Сла́ва Бо́гу! о́чень хорошо́,	slàhva bòhoo!òtchen kharashò.
I am well,	Я здоро́въ,	ya zdaròf.
I am very heappy to hear it,	Я э́тому ра́дуюсь,	ya aitamoo ràdooyouss.
I am not well,	Я не та́къ-то здоро́въ,	ya nai tak-to zdaròf.
I am sorry for it,	Я о́чень сожалѣ́ю,	ya òtchen sazhaileyou.
What do you wish?	Чего́ изво́лите?	tchevò eezòleete?
What do you like?	Что вамъ уго́дно?	shto vam oogòdno?

What do ask for?	Что ты хо́чешь?	shto tee khòtchesh?
Will you take?	Изво́лите ли?	eezvòleete lee?
Will you have?	Хо́чешь ли?	khòtchesh lee?
Will you take a knife (a plate)?	Изво́лите ли но́жикъ (таре́лку)?	eezvòleete lee nòzheek (taraìlkoo)?
Shall I help you to some bread?	Хо́чешь ли хлѣ́ба?	khòtchesh lee khlaiba?
Yes, Sir; I pray you,	Да, су́дарь; я васъ прошу́,	da, soòdar; ya vass prashoò.
No, Ma'am (Miss), I thank you,	Нѣтъ, суда́рыня, благодарю́ васъ,	n'yett, soodàhreenia, blagadaroù vass.
It is not necessary,	Не на́добно,	nai nàdobno.
Give me,	Пода́й мнѣ; пода́йте мнѣ,	padày mnai; padàyte mnai.
Give me, if you please,	Пожа́луйте мнѣ,	pahzàlueete mnai.
Do be so kind as to give me,	Пожа́луй мнѣ,	pazhàluy mnai.
Give me a pen and ink,	Пода́йте мнѣ перо́ и чернѝла,	padàyte mnai pairò ee tcherneèla.
Give me, if you please, a small glass of brandy,	Пожа́луйте мнѣ рю́мку во́дки.	pazhàluyte mnai r'youmkoo vòdkee.
Give me the key (my boots),	Пода́й мнѣ ключъ, (сапоги́),	padày mnai klyootch (sapagheè).
Reach here,	Пода́й сюда́,	padày soodà.
Pray, I pray you.	Прошу́,	prashoò.
Be so kind as,	Сдѣ́лайте ми́лость,	zdyaìlàyte meèlost.
Excuse me,	Извини́те,	eezveeneèle.
Presently, Sir,	То́тчасъ, (сей часъ), су́дарь,	tòtchass (seytchass), soòdar.
Tell me, if you please,	Скажи́те мнѣ, пожа́луйста,	skazheèle mnai, pazhàluysta.
I beg pardon for interrupting you,	Извини́те, что я перебью́ ва́шу рѣчь,	eezveeneèle shto ya perebyoù vàshoo raitch.
You will oblige me exceedingly,	Вы меня́ весьма́ одолжи́те,	wee men'yà vesmà adalzeèle.

Do me this pleasure,	Сдѣлайте мнѣ это удовóльствіе,	zdailéytai mnai aito oodavòlstviay.
When you please,	Когдá вамъ угóдно бýдетъ,	kagdàh vam oogòdno boòdet.
Willingly,	Охóтно,	akhòtno.
I am at your disposal,	Я къ вáшимъ услý-гамъ,	ya k' vàsheem oosloogam.
I thank you,	Благодáрствую,	blagadàrstvooyou.
Where is (are)?	Гдѣ?	gdai.
Where is my room?	Гдѣ моя кóмпата?	gdai mayà kòmnata?
Where are the servants?	Гдѣ люди?	gdai léwdee?
Here they are, Sir,	Здѣсь они, сýдарь,	zdaiss aneè, soòdar.
Here she is, Miss,	Вотъ онá, судá-рыня!	vott auàh, soodàreenya.
Will you go up to your room?	Извóлите ли итти въ вáшу кóмнату?	eezvòleetai lee eetteè v' vàshoo kòmnatoo?
Not yet,	Нѣтъ ещё,	nait ycshtchò.
After,	Пóслѣ,	pòslai.
Do you keep a table d'hôte?	Держите ли вы óбщій стóлъ?	derzheètai lee wee òbshtchee stoll?
So much the better,	Тѣмъ лýчше,	taim loòishai.
At what o' clock do they sup at your house?	Въ котóромъ часý ýжипаютъ у васъ?	f' katòrom tchassoò oozheenàyout oo vass?
Can you accommodate us with lodging for this night?	Мóжете ли вы при-пять насъ эту ночь?	mòzhaitai lee wee preenyàtt nass aitoo notch?
I'd wish to have a room with two beds,	Мнѣ хотѣлось бы кóмнату съ двумя кровáтями,	mnai khataìloss bwe kòmnatoos' dvoomà kravàtamee.
Is the bed made?	Перестлапá ли по-стéль?	pairaistlanà lee pastail?
I go with you,	Я пойдý съ вáми,	ya paydoòs' vàmee.
Very well,	О'чень хорошó,	òtchain kharashò.
Good night,	Дóбрая ночь, (прощáйте),	dòbraya notch (prashtchèytai).

46

Sleep well,	Почивайте спокойно,	patcheevéytai spakòyno.
And you likewise,	И вы также,	ee we tàkzhai.
See that my carriage is put in the coach-house,	Прикажите поставить карету мою въ сарай,	preekazheètai pastàveet karaìtoo mayoù v' sarèy.
I'll be answerable for every thing,	Я вамъ за всё отвѣчаю,	ya vam za fsyò atvaitchàyou.
I will sup (dine) in my room,	Я буду ужинать (обѣдать) въ своей комнатѣ,	ya boòdoo oòzheenat (abaìdat) v' svayèy kòmnatai.
Have you any other orders to give?	Не прикажете ли ещё чего?	nai preekàzhaitai lee yeshtchò tshaivò?
Awake me early tomorrow,	Прикажите разбудить меня завтра поранье,	preekazheètai razboodeét menyà zàftra paranaiyai.
Can the door be locked?	Дверь запирается ли ключёмъ?	dvair zapeeràyetsa lee klootchòm?

DIALOGUE II.

How is this street called?	Какъ называется эта улица?	kak nazeevàyetsa aita oòleetsa?
The perspective of Nevsky,	Невский Проспектъ,	naìfskee praspèkt.
The great Millionne,	Большая Миллионная,	balshàya milliònnaya.
The little Morskoy,	Малая Морская,	màlaya marskàya.
The Galleys street,	Галерная улица,	galèrnaya oòlitsa.
The English quay,	А'нглийская нáбережная,	àngleeskaya nàbairaizhnaya.
And that bridge?	А этотъ мостъ?	a aitott most?
It is the bridge of Nicholas,	Это Николаевский мостъ,	aito neekolàyefskee most.
Could you tell me,	Знаете ли вы гдѣ	znàyaitai lee we gdai

where Mr N. lives?	живётъ госпо-дйнъ N?	zheeviòtt gaspadeèn N?
I don't know,	Не знаю,	nai znàyou.
Where is the porter?	Гдѣ дворникъ?	gdai dvòrneek
Good morning, porter (my dear)!	Здравствуй, дворникъ (братъ)!	zdràstvuy, dvòrneek, (bratt)!
Is there any body here who can speak French (German or English)?	Не говоритъ ли здѣсь кто пофранцу́зски (понѣмѐцки, или поа́нглійски)?	nai gavareèt lee zdaiss khto pafrantzoòskee (panaimaìtskee, eeleè pa-àngleeskee)?
He will come presently,	Онъ сей часъ придётъ,	onn sey tchass preedyòtt.
Is it here that Mr. N. lives?	Живётъ ли здѣсь господйнъ N?	zheeviòtt lee zdaiss gaspadeèn N?
Is Mister N. (Madam or Miss) at home?	Дома ли господйнъ N. (госпожа́ N.)?	dòma lee gaspadeèn N.(gaspazhàhN)?
He (she) is at home,	Дома, (онъ, она дома),	dòma, (onn, anàh dòma).
He (she) is not at home,	Нѣтъ его́ (ея) дома,	naitt yevò (yeyò) dòma.
There is nobody at home,	Никого́ дома нѣтъ,	neekavò dòma naitt.
He went out (a foot, in a coach),	Онъ пошёлъ, (поѣхалъ) со двора́,	onn pashòll (payaìkhall) sa dvaràh.
Hold here are twenty kopecks; accompany me to his house,	Вотъ тебѣ два́дцать копѣекъ; отведи́ меня къ нему́,	votttaibaidvàtsat kapaìyaik; atvaideè menà k' nemoò.
Wait a moment,	Подожди́те немно́го,	padazhdeètai naimnògo.
Go and see if he is still at home,	Поди́, посмотри́ дома ли онъ ещё,	padeè, pasmatreè dòma lee onn yeshtchò.
I will wait here,	Я здѣсь подожду́,	ya zdaiss padazhdoò.
When does he return?	Когда́ онъ бу́детъ домой?	kagdàh onn boòdait damòy?

At three o' clock,	Въ три часа́,	f' tree tchassàh.
At past three o' clock,	Въ четвёртомъ часу́,	f' tchaitvyòrtom tchassoò.
Is it long since he went out?	Давно́ ли онъ пошёлъ со двора́ (вы́шелъ)?	davnò lee on pashòll sa dvaràh (weèshail)?
He started at two o' clock for the exchange,	Онъ пое́халъ на би́ржу въ два часа́,	onn payaikhall na beèrzhoo v' dva tchassàh.
I'll wait for his return,	Я подожду́, поку́да онъ воро́тится,	ya padazhdoò, pakoòda onn varòteetsa.
I'll come again,	Я опя́ть приду́,	ya opàt preedoò.
At what o' clock?	Въ кото́ромъ часу́?	f' katòrom tchassoò?
At half past five,	Въ полови́нѣ шеста́го,	f' palaveènai shaistòva.
Hold here is drink-money,	Вотъ тебѣ́ на во́дку,	vott taibai na vòdkoo.
Adieu, my friend,	Проща́й, бра́тъ,	prashtchèy, braht.
Whence are you coming?	Отку́да вы идёте?	atkoòda we eedyòtai?
I am coming from my house (my garden),	Я иду́ и́зъ дому (изъ са́да),	ya eedoò èez damoo (eez sàhda).
Where are you going to?	Куда́ вы идёте?	koòda we eedyòtai?
I am going home,	Я иду́ домо́й,	ya eedoò damòy.
Where do you live?	Гдѣ вы живёте?	gdai we zheevyòtai?
In the street of the gardens.	Въ садо́вой у́лицѣ,	f' sadòvoy oòleetsai.
In the officers' street,	Въ офицёрской у́лицѣ,	v' afeetsèrskoy oòleetsai.
On the quay,	По на́бережной,	pa nàbairaizhnoy.
On the Catherine canal,	По Екатери́нскому кана́лу,	pa yekatereènskomoo kanàloo.
At Wassily-Ostrof,	На Васи́льевскомъ острову́,	na vasseèliefskom astravoò.
In what house and	Въ кото́ромъ до́-	f' katòrom dòmai ee

what number?	мѣ и подъ ка-кймъ нóмеромъ?	pad kakeém nò-mairom?
In Mr N. 's house, at the number,	Въ дóмѣ Госпо-дйна N. подъ нó-меромъ,	v' dòmai gaspadeèna N. pad nòmairom.
Good day (morning, night), Sir, (Ma' am, Miss)!	Прощáйте!	prashtchèytai!
Till we meet again.	До свидáнія,	da sveedàneea.

DIALOGUE III.

Can you tell me which way I am to go to arrive at my dwelling?	Не мóжете ли вы сказáть мнѣ, ка-кóю дорóгою дойтй мнѣ до моéй квартйры?	nai mòzhaitai lee we skazàt mnai ka-kòyou darògoyou daeeteè mnai da mayèy kvarteè-ree?
Show me your bill,	Покажйте мнѣ вашъ билéтъ,	pakazheètai mnai vàsh beelètt.
Here it is,	Вотъ онъ,	vott on.
Go straight before you,	Ступáйте всё пря-мо,	stoopàytai fsyo prà-mo.
Now you will turn on your left hand,	Теперь налѣво,	taipair nalaivo.
Afterwards on the right,	А потóмъ напрáво,	a patòm npràvo.
Here it your dwel-ling,	Вотъ вáша квар-тйра,	vott vàsha kvarteèra.
Is the Master (Mis-tress) of the house at home?	Дóма ли бáринъ, хозяинъ (бáры-ня, хозяйка)?	dòma lee bàhrinn, khazyàeen (bàh-reenia, khazeeày-ka)?
Show me to my room,	Покажйте мнѣ мою кóмнату,	pakazheètai mnai mayoù kòmnatoo.
Come with me, little boy,	Подй со мной, мáльчикъ,	padeè sa mnoy, màl-tcheek.

4

Here is your room,	Вотъ ваша комната,	voll vàsha kòmnata.
I thank you,	Спасибо,	spasseèbo.
It is not worth mentioning,	Нé за что,	nai za shto.
There is a table, a chair and a candlestick,	Вотъ вамъ столъ, стулъ и шандалъ (подсвѣчникъ),	voll vam stol, stool ee shandàll (padsvaìshneek).
You are tired?	Устали ли вы?	oostàlee lee we?
I am not tired,	Я совсѣмъ не усталъ,	ya safsaìm nai oostàll.
You are a good fellow,	Ты добрый малый,	tee dòbree màlee.
The Russians are worthy people,	Русскіе добрые люди (добрый народъ),	rooskeeyai dòbreeai lèwdee (dòbree naròtt).
They are friends,	Они наши братья,	aneè nàshee bràtya.
Do you speak French (Russian)?	Говорите ли вы по-французски (по-русски)?	gavareètai lee we pa -frantsoòskee (pa-roòskee)?
Yes; I am a Frenchman (Russian),	Говорю; я французъ (русскій),	gavaroò; ya frantsooz (roòskee).
Not too much,	Немного,	naimnògo.
Very little,	О́чень мало,	òtchen màlo.
Do you understand what I say?	Разумѣете ли вы то, что я говорю?	razoomaìyaitai lee we to, shto ya gavaroò?
I understand it,	Разумѣю,	razoomaìyou.
Very well,	О́чень разумѣю,	òtchen razoomaìyou.
I do not (don't) understand it,	Не разумѣю,	nai razoomaìyou.
I don't understand a word of it,	Ничего не разумѣю,	neetchaivò nai razoomaiyou.
Do not speak so fast, if you please,	Пожалуйста, не говорите такъ скоро,	pazhàluista, nai gavareètai tak skòro.
Speak slowly,	Говорите тихо(потише),	gavareètai teèkho (pateèshai).
Still more slowly,	Ещё потише,	yeshtchò pateéshai.

What is your name?	Какъ васъ зовутъ?	kak vass zavoòt?
How do you call yourself?	Какъ тебя зовутъ?	kak taibà zavoòt?
I am called Nicholas,	Я называюсь Ни-колаемъ,	ya nazeevàyouss neekalàyem.
My name is Nicholas (John 's son),	Меня зовутъ Ни-колаемъ Ивано-вичемъ,	mainà zavoòt neeka-làyem cevànovee-tchem.
What' s the name of this in Russian (in German)?	Какъ это называ-ется по-русски (по-нѣмецки)?	kak aìto nazeevà-yetsa pa-roòskee (pa-naimètskee)?
Adieu! God direct you!	Прощай! Богъ съ тобою?	prashtchèy! bokh s' tabòyou!

DIALOGUE IV.

At what o' clock do you dine?	Въ которомъ часу обѣдаете вы?	f' katòrom tchassoò abaìdayaite we?
At four o' clock,	Въ четыре часа,	f' tchaiteèrai tchassà.
Is dinner ready?	Готово ли ку-шанье?	gatòvo lee koòsha-neeyai?
Dinner is on the table,	Кушанье подано (на столѣ),	koòshaneeyai pòda-no (na stalaì).
Let us sit down to table,	Сядемъ за столъ,	syàdaim za stoll.
Sit down here,	Садитесь здѣсь,	sadeètess zdaiss.
What do you please to want?	Угодно ли вамъ?	oogòdno lee vam?
Help yourself,	Извольте брать,	eezvòltai brat.
After you, Ma' am,	Послѣ васъ, су-дарыня,	pòslai vass, soodà-reenya.
You eat nothing,	Вы не кушаете?	we nai koòshayaitai?
Drink a glass,	Пейте,	pèytai.
I have dined very heartily,	Я ѣлъ довольно,	ya yaill davòlno.
You have a mind to make me tipsy,	Вы хотите меня подпоить,	we khateètai mainà padpaeèt.

4*

Do not be afraid,	Не опасайтесь,	nai apasséytaiss.
This wine is not heady,	Это вино не крѣпко,	aito veenò nai kraipko.
Your health, gentlemen,	За ваше здравіе, господа,	za vàshai zdràveeyai, ghaspadà.
Your good health,	II за ваше,	ee za vàshai.
Let us rise from table, if you please,	Встанемъ, если, угодно, изъ-за стола,	fstàuaim, yèslee oogòdno, eez - za stalàh.
Willingly,	Я согласенъ,	ya saglàssen.

DIALOGUE V.

Where is the inn, the city of London?	Гдѣ гостинница, городъ .Лондонъ?	gdai ghasteèneetsa, gòrod lòndon ?
Opposite the admiralty; near the boulevard,	Противъ адмиралтейства; подлѣ булевара,	pròteef admeeraltèystva; pòdlai boolaivàra.
And the hotel of Demout?	II отель Демута?	ee òtel daimoota ?
On the great stable-street,	Въ Большой Конюшенной,	v' balshòy kanyoùshennoy.
Can we lodge here?	Можно ли намъ прпстать у васъ?	mòzhno lee nam preestàl oo vass?
Have you any rooms to let?	Есть ли у васъ квартира?	yest lee oo vass kvarteèra ?
On what days does the post leave for Moscow?	Когда идётъ почта въ Москву?	kaghdà eediòtt pòtshta v' maskvoò ?
What day of the month is it?	Которое сего дня число?	katòroyai saivò dnee tcheeslò ?
Send that letter in the post-office,	Пошлите это письмо на почту,	pashleètè aito peesmò na pòtchtoo.
Here is my passport,	Вотъ мой пашпортъ,	vott moy pàshport.
Do be so kind as to	Пожалуйста, ска-	pazhaluysta, ska-

tell me where the custom-house is?	жи́те мнѣ гдѣ тамо́жня,	zheétai mnai, gdai tamòzhna.
Do me this favour,	Сдѣлайте мнѣ ми́лость,	zdailèytai mnai meélost.
I cannot,	Я не могу́,	ya nai magoò.
I have not time,	Не имѣю вре́мени, (мнѣ не досу́гъ),	nai eemaiyou vraimenee, (mnai nai dassoòg).
I request of you to tell me,	Прошу́ поко́рно,	prashoò pakòrno.
It is impossible,	Нельзя́,	nailzà.
Excuse me,	Извини́те меня́,	cezveencèle mainà.
Is it true?	Пра́вда ли?	pràvda lee?
Is it so?	Такъ ли?	tak lee?
Yes, it is true,	Пра́вда,	pràvda.
Truly,	Пра́во (въ са́момъ дѣлѣ),	pràvo (v' sàhmom dailai).
Without doubt,	Безъ сомнѣнія,	bez somnainya.
I have forgotten it,	Я позабы́лъ,	ya pazabwcèl.
Do no forget,	Не забыва́йте, (не забу́дьте),	nai zabwevèytai, (nai zaboòdtai).
I cannot recollect it,	Я не могу́ припо́мнить,	ya nai magoò preepòmneet.
I have a sad memory,	У меня́ па́мять слаба́,	oo mainà pàmat slabà.
What are you looking for?	Чего́ вы и́щете?	tchevò we eéshtchaitai ?
I am looking for my hat,	Я ищу́ мое́й шля́пы,	ya eeshtchoò mayèy shlyàpwee.
My gloves,	Мои́хъ перча́токъ,	maeèkh pairtchàtok.
See here they are,	Вотъ она́ (онѣ́),	vott anà, (anai).
Here are your letters,	Вотъ ва́ши пи́сьма,	vott vàshee peèsma.
Mister N. is asking after you,	Господи́нъ N. васъ спра́шиваетъ,	gaspadìnn N. vass spràsheevayet.
Request of him to walk in?	Попроси́ его́ сюда́,	paprasseè yevò soodà.

DIALOGUE VI.

How fare may it be from here to Tzarskoe Selo?	Далёко ли отсюда до Царскаго Села?	dalyòko lee atsoòda da tzàrskava sailà?
Is the road good?	Хороша ли дорога?	kharashà lee daròga?
It is very good (bad),	О'чень хороша (дурна),	òtchen karashà (doornà).
Are we still fare from the town?	Что далёко ещё до города?	shto dalyòko yeshtchò dò garada?
Which is the best inn in the town?	Какой трактиръ лучше всѣхъ въ городѣ?	kakòy trakteèr loòtchai fsaikh v' gòrodai?
Come, make haste, postilion,	Ну! ступай проворнѣе, ямщикъ,	noo! stoopèy pravornaìyai, yemshtcheèk.
I am in a hurry to arrive at,	Я спѣшу доѣхать,	ya spaishoò dayaikhat.
If you drive well, I will double the drink-money,	Е'сли ты меня повезёшь поскорѣе, то прибавлю тебѣ на водку,	yèslee tee menà pavézyòsh paskaraìyai, to preebàvlew taibai na vòdkoo.
Stop, you are going to upset,	Тише! опрокинешь,	teèshai! aprakeènaish.
I will get down here,	Я здѣсь сойду,	ya zdaiss şèydoo.
Open the door and let down the steps,	Отвори двѣрцы и опусти подножку,	atvareè dvaìrtsee ee apoosteè padnòshkoo.
Stop!	Стой (остановись)!	stoy! (astanaveèss)!
How is the weather?	Какова погода?	kakavà pagòda?
It is fine weather (bad weather),	Погода прекрасная (дурная),	pagòda praikràsnaya (doornàya).
It is day,	Разсвѣтаетъ,	razsvaitàyett.
It is night,	Ночь на дворѣ,	notch na dvaraì.
It is cold (hot),	Холодно, (тепло),	khòlodno, (taiplò).
I am very warm,	Мнѣ очень жарко,	mnai òtchen zhàrko.
I am cold,	Я озябъ,	ya azyàb.

It freezes,	Мёрзнетъ,	myòrznait.
The river is frozen,	Рѣка̀ замёрзла,	raikà zamyòrzla,
	(встала),	(ftàla).
It snows,	Снѣгъ идётъ,	snaik eediòtt.
It is windy,	Вѣтряно,	vaitréno.
The wind has chan-	Вѣтръ перемѣ-	vaitr pairaimaineèl-
ged,	ни́лся,	sa.
It thaws,	Стала о́ттепель,	stàla òttaipail.
The ice is breaking	Iёдъ пошёлъ,	lyott pashòll.
up,		
The mist ascends,	Тума́нъ поднима̀-	toomàn padneemà-
	ется,	yetsa.
The weather is very	Э'та зима̀ дово́льно	aìta zeemà davòlno
cold this winter,	моро́зна,	maròzna.
Did it freeze?	Моро́зило ли?	maròzeelo lee?
It is going to rain,	Дождь сбира́ется,	dòzhd zbeeràyetsa.
It rains,	До́ждикъ идётъ,	dòzhzheek eedyòtt.
It pours with rain,	Дождь пошёлъ	dòzhd pashòll pra-
	проливно́й,	leevnòy.
It hails,	Идётъ гра́дъ,	eedyòtt grad.
The weather is stor-	Подыма́ется гроза̀,	padcemàyetsa gra-
my,		zàh.
It is very dusty,	О'чень пы́льно,	òtchen pweèlno.
The weather begins	Пого́да прочища̀-	pagòda pratcheesh-
to settle,	ется,	tchàyetsa.
It thunders,	Громъ греми́тъ,	grom graimeèt.
It lightens,	Мо́лнія сверка́етъ,	mòlneeya sverkàyett.
Ah! how warm it is?	Ахъ! какъ жа́рко!	akh, kak zhàrko!
I am stifled with the	Я задыха́юсь отъ	ya zadeekhàyouss at
heat,	жа́ру,	zhàroo.
The thunderbolt has	Мо́лнія уда́рила,	mòlneeya oodàreela.
fallen,		
The storm is over,	Бу́ря ути́хла,	boòra ooteèkhla.
It is very dirty,	Гря́зно на дворѣ̀,	gràzno na dvaraì.
The sun is rising (is	Со́лнце восхо́дитъ,	sòntsai vaskhòdeet,
setting),	(захо́дитъ),	(zakhòdeet).
It is dreadful wea-	Пого́да са́мая	pagòda sàhmaya
ther,	скве́рная,	skvairnaya.

The days are growing shorter (longer),	Дни ужé убавляются (прибавляются),	dnee oozhai oobavlàyoutsa, (preebavlàyoutsa).
Let us go and take a walk,	Пойдёмте прогýливаться,	peydyòmtai pragoòleevatsa.
Willingly,	Я соглáсепъ,	ya saglàssen.
Which way shall we go?	Кудá жъ намъ птти́?	koodàzh nam eetteè?
Which way you please,	Кудá вамъ угóдно,	koodà vam oogòdno.
We will go to the summer garden,	Пойдёмте въ лѣтпій садъ,	peydyòmtai v'laitnee sad.
To the island of Krestofsky,	На Крестóвскій óстровъ,	na kraistòfskee òstrof.
To the garden of plants,	На аптéкарскій óстровъ,	na aptaikarskee òstrof.
To the boulevard,	На булевáръ,	na boolevàr.
Are you tired?	Устáли ли вы?	oostàlee lee we?
I am not tired; let us continne our walk,	Я не устáлъ; стáпемъ продолжáть нáшу прогýлку,	ya nai oostàll; stànaime pradalzhàt nàshoo pragoòlkoo.
Let us rest a little on the grass (on the bench),	Отдохнёмъ пемнóго на дёрпѣ, (на лáвкѣ),	atdakhnyòm naimnògo na dyòrnai, (na làfkai).
Let us return home,	Ворóтимся домóй,	varòteemsa damòy.
As you please,	Какъ вамъ угóдпо,	kak vam oogòdno.
Ho, porter! open the door,	Эй, двóрникъ! отворú ворóта,	ey, dvòrneek, atvareè varòta.
Light me,	Посвѣтú мнѣ,	pasvaiteè mnai.
Walk before,	Ступáй впéредъ,	stoopèy fpairòd.
Open my door,	Отопрú дверь мою́,	atapreè dvair mayoù.
Shut the window,	Затворú окóшко,	zatvareè akòshko.
What o'clock is it?	Котóрый часъ?	katòree tchass?
It is midnight,	Двѣнáдцатьчасóвъ,	dvainàtsat tchassòf.
It has struck one,	Чáсъ бúло,	tchass beèlo.
It is two o'clock,	Два часá, (трéтій часъ),	dva tchassà, (traitee tchass).
It is past five o'clock,	Шестóй часъ,	chaistòy tchass.

It is half past eight,	Половина девятаго	palaveèna devàtava.
It is a quarter past ten,	Четверть одиннадцатаго,	tchaìtvert adeénnatstatava.
It is a quarter to eleven.	Трп четвертп одиннадцатаго,	Tree tchaìtvertee adeennàtsatava.
To-morrow morning at seven o' clock,	Завтра по утру въ семь часовъ,	zàftra pa ootroò v' saim tchassòf.
Take my boots (my shoes) to clean them,	Возьми вычистить мой сапоги (башмаки),	vazmeè wcetcheesteet maeè sapagheè (bashmakeè).
Send me the hairdresser (barber) very early,	Пошли ко мнѣ парикмахера (цирюльпика), завтра порапѣе,	pashleé ka mnai pareekmàkhéra (tseerùlnecka), zàftra parànayai.
Take care not to forget it,	Только не позабудь,	tòlko nai pazaboòd.
I will not fail to do so, Sir,	Слушаю, сударь, (слушаюсь),	sloòshayou, soòdar, (sloòshayouss).

DIALOGUE VII.

The barber is come,	Цирюльппкъ пришёлъ, (здѣсь),	tseerùlneek preeshòll (zdaiss).
You seem to be in no great hurry to-day, friend,	Ты, братъ, застáвилъ сего дпя долго себя дожидать,	tee, bràt, zastàveel saivò dnee dòlgo saibà dazheedàt.
Come, make haste and shave me,	Ну, поскорѣй! выбрѣй меня,	noo, paskarèy! weèbrey mainà.
There is the shaving dish and the soap-ball,	Вотъ брильное блюдце п мыло,	vot brcèlnoyai blùdtsai ee mweèlo.
Make haste; I want to go out,	Проворпѣе же; мнѣ надобпо иттй,	pravòrnayai zhai, mnaɪnàdobno eetteè.
Your razor does not cut well,	Твоя бритва пе брѣетъ,	tvayà breètva nai braìyett.

58

You have not soaped the beard enough,	Ты не довóльно намылилъ бóроду,	tee nai davòlno namweèleel bòrodoo.
There you are shaved,	Вотъ и готóво,	voit ee gatòvo.
Give me the napkin to wipe myself,	Подáй мнѣ полотéнце осушѝться,	padéy mnai palatèntse assooheètsa.
Cut my hair,	Подстригѝ мнѣ вóлосы,	padstreegheè mnai vòlossee.
Now comb me a little	Тепéрь причешѝ меня,	taipair preetchaisheé mainà.
My hair does not curl sufficiently,	Вóлосы у меня не завивáются,	vòlossee oo menà nai zaveevàyoutsa.
Hold, there's a rouble for your trouble,	Вотъ тебѣ рубль за труды,	vott taibai roobl za troodcè.

DIALOGUE VIII.

Who knocks at the door?	Кто стучѝтся у дверéй?	khto stoòtcheetsa oo dvairèy?
Who is there?	Кто тамъ?	khto tam?
Come (walk) in,	Войдѝте,	voydeète.
The boy is come,	Артéльщикъ пришёлъ,	artailshtcheek preeshòll.
Come here,	Подѝ сюдá,	padeè soodà.
Who sent you?	Кто тебя послáлъ?	khto taibà paslàll.
Wait a moment,	Подождѝ (погодѝ) немнóго,	padazhdeè (pagadeè) naimnògo.
I will give you a note,	Я дамъ тебѣ запѝску,	ya dam taibai apeèskoo.
Bring me some bread,	Принесѝ мнѣ хлѣба,	preenesseè mnai khlaìba.
Prepare my breakfast,	Приготóвь мнѣ зáвтракъ,	preegotòve mnai zàftrak.
Give me a pipe,	Подáй мнѣ трýбку,	padey mnai troòbkoo.
Light the candle,	Засвѣтѝ свѣчý,	zasvaiteè svaitchoò.

Heat my stove,	Затопи печь (печку),	zatapeè paitch (paitchkoo).
Make a fire,	Разведи огонь,	razvaideè agòn.
Give me the bason and soap,	Подай рукомойникъ и мыла,	padèy rookamòyneek ee mweèla.
Leave me,	Ступай теперь,	stoopèy taipair.
Go faster,	Ступай скорѣе (проворпье),	stoopèy skarèy (pravòrney).
Stop!	Стой (постой)!	stoy (pastòy)!
Here is the washer-woman coming,	Вотъ прачка пришла,	vott pràtchka preeshlà.
Do you want her?	Надобна ли она вамъ?	nàdobna lee anàh vam?
Yes; I want clean linen,	Да; мнѣ надобно чистое бѣльё,	da; mnai nadobno tcheéstoyai bailyò.
Go and fetch me a droshky (a sledge),	Поди, достань мнѣ дрожки, (сани),	padeè, dastàn mnai dròshkee, (sànee).
How much do you ask of me?	Сколько просишь?	skòlko pròssish?
Eighty kopecks,	Восемь гривенъ,	vòsaim greèven.
It is too dear,	Это очень дорого,	aito òtchen dòrogo.
I will give no more than sixty kopecks for it,	Не дамъ болѣе шести гривенъ,	nai dam bòlaiyai shaisteè greèven.
Well! get up, Sir,	Хорошо! садитесь, сударь,	kharashò! sadeètaiss, soòdar.
Drive fast,	Ступай проворнье,	stoopèy pravòrney.
Stop, coachman! we are arrived,	Стой, извощикъ! мы доѣхали,	stoy, eezvòstcheek! mwe dayaìkkalee.

DIALOGUE IX.

I'd wish to see the curiosities of the city,	Мнѣ хотѣлось бы посмотрѣть рѣдкости города,	mnai khatailoss bwe pasmatraìt raìdkostee gòroda.

Here is a footman hired by the day, who will show you the way,	Вотъ паёмный слуга васъ проведётъ,	vott nayómnee sloogà vass pravaidyòtt.
Take me to the church of Kazan,	Поведи меня въ Казанскую церковь,	pravaideè mainà v' Kazànskooyou tsairkov.
What is curious to be seen there?	Что тамъ есть любопытнаго?	shto tam yest lewbapweètnava?
It contains a great number of standards taken from the enemy and other trophies,	Тамъ хранятся многія знамена, отнятыя у непріятеля и другіе трофеи,	tam khranàtsa mnòghia znamainàh, atnateèya oo naipreeyàtela, ee droogheèyai trafaiee.
Let us go and see the monument of Peter the Great,	Пойдёмте посмотрѣть памятникъ Петру Великому,	peydyòmtai pasmatraite pàmetneek petroò vaileèkomoo.
The column of Alexander,	Александровскую колонну,	alexandròfskooyou kalònnoo.
The marbre palace,	Мраморный дворецъ,	mràmornee dvaraits.
The museum,	Кунсткамеру,	koonst kàmairoo.
The Imperial library,	Императорскую библіотеку,	eempairàtorskooyou beeblyòtaikoo.
The Academy of fine arts,	Академію Художествъ,	akadaìmeeyou khoodòzhaistv.
The new exchange,	Новую биржу,	nòvooyou beérzhoo.
The Lombard,	Ломбардъ,	lambàrd.
The St-Michael's palace,	Михайловскій замокъ,	meekhèylofskee zàmok.
The new bridge on the Neva,	Новый мостъ на Невѣ,	nòwee most na naivaì.
Let us cross over the bridge,	Перейдёмъ мостъ,	paireydyòm most.
What an imposing aspect!	Какой величественный видъ!	kakòy vaileètchaistvennce veed!

This flat bridge is magnificent,	Э́тотъ плóскій мостъ великолѣ́пенъ,	aìtot plòskee most vaileekolaipen.
Let us go on the quay in order to see the whole to greater advantage,	Пойдёмте по нáбережной, чтóбы лýчше обозрѣ́ть всё,	peydyòmtai pa nàbairezhnoy, shtobwee loòtchai abazrait fsyo.
The city follows the course of the river,	Гóродъ пострóенъ вдоль рѣки́,	gòrod pastròyen vdol raikeè.
What is the circumference of the city?	Какъ велйкъ гóродъ въ окрýжности?	kak vaileèk gòrod v' okroòzhnostec?
Now accompany me to my dwelling,	Тепéрь проводи́ меня́ опя́ть домóй,	taipair pravadeè mainà apait damòy.
Get me newspapers,	Достáнь мнѣ газéтъ,	dastàn mnai gazait.
What gazettes appear here?	Какíя выхóдятъ здѣсь газéты?	kakeèya weekhòdat zdaiss gazaitee?
The gazette of St-Petersburg,	Петербýргскія вѣ́домости,	peterboòrgskeeya vaidomostee.
The Russian Invalid, or military gazette,	Рýсскій Инвали́дъ, или вое́нныя вѣ́домости,	roòskie eenvaleèd, eeleè vayènneeya vaidomostee.
The Northern Bee,	Сѣ́верная Пчелá,	saivernaya ptchailà.
And the gazette of the Senate,	И Сенáтскія вѣ́домости,	ee sainàtskeeya vaidomostee.
Are there reading-rooms here?	Есть ли здѣсь библіóтеки для чтéнія?	yest lee zdaiss bee-blyòtaikce dla tchtainia?
There are six,	Здѣсь шесть такóвыхъ,	zdaiss shaist takaweekh.
The French literary saloons of Mr Loury in the house of St-Peter's church, and of Mr Issakof in the great bazar,	Зáлы для францýзскаго чтéнія Господи́на Лýри, въ дóмѣ Петровской Цéркви, и Г-на Исáкова,	zàlee dla frantzoùsskava tchtaineeya gaspadeèna loòree, v' dòmai petròfskoy sairkvee, ee gaspodcèna

	въ гостнномъ дворѣ,	eesàkova, v' ghasteènom dvaraì.
TheGermanreading-rooms of Mr Schmitzdorf, at the great Morskoy street, and of Mr Höwert, on the perspective of Nevsky,	Библіótеки для нѣмéцкаго чтéнія Господнна Шмнцдорфа, въ большóй Морскóй, и Г-па Гёверта, на Нéвскомъ Проспéктѣ,	beeblyòtaikee dla naimaìtskava ichtaìnya gaspadeèna shmeètzdorfa, v' balshòy marskòy, ee gaspadeèna haìvairta, na naìfskom praspaìktai.
And the Russian reading-rooms of Mr Smirdin, on the Michael place, and of Mr Glazoonof, at the gardens' street,	II библіótеки для рýсскаго чтéнія Господнна Смнрднна, на Михáйловской плóщади, и Г-па Глазупóва, въ Садóвой ýлицѣ,	ee beeblyòtaikee dla roòskava ichtaìnya gaspadeèna smeèrdeena, na meekhèylofskoy plòshtchadee, ee gaspadeèna glazoonòva, v' sadòvoy oòleetsai.
Subscriptions may be taken for one year, for six, three and even one month,	Тамъ подпнсываются нá годъ, нá шесть, нá три мѣсяца, и дáже на (однпъ) мѣсяцъ,	tam padpeèseeva-youtsa nà god, nà shaist, nà tree maìsaitsa, ee dàzhai na (adeèn) maissats.
Which are the churches for foreign confessions?	Какія здѣсь цéрквн для ннострáнныхъ вѣроисповѣданій?	kakeèya zdaiss tsaìrkvee dla eenastrànneekh vairoeezpavaìdanee?
The lutherian churches,	Лютерáнскія цéрквн,	lutairànskeeya tsaìrkvee,
St-Peter's,	Святáго Петрá,	svaitòva paitrà.
St-Anne's,	Святыя Áнны,	svaiteèya ànnee.
St-Catherine's,	Святыя Екатернны,	svaiteèya yekatereènee.
The catholic church,	Католнческая цéрковь,	kataleètchaiskaya tsaìrkov.

63

Thereformed church,	Реформа́тская це́рковь,	raifarmàtskaya tsairkov,
For the French,	Для Францу́зовъ,	dla frantzoòzof.
For the Dutch,	Для Голла́ндцевъ,	dla gallàndtsaif.
For the Germans,	Для Не́мцевъ,	dla naimtsaif,
For the English,	Для Англича́нъ,	dla angleetchàn.
For the Moravian brothers,	Для Мора́вскихъ бра́тьевъ,	dla moràfskeekh bràhtyef.
A Swedish church,	Шве́дская це́рковь,	shvaìdskaya tsairkof.
A Finnish church,	Чухо́пская (Фи́н-ская) це́рковь,	tchookhònskaya (feénskaya) tsairkof.
And lastly an Armenian church,	И наконе́цъ Армя́нская це́рковь,	ee nakanàits armyànskaya tsairkof.

DIALOGUE X.

Do you know Mister N?	Зна́ете ли вы Госпо́дина N?	znàyaitai lee wee gaspadeèna N?
Yes, Sir, I know him,	Да, су́дарь, зна́ю,	da, soòdar, znàyou.
No, Sir, I don't know him,	Нѣтъ, су́дарь, я его́ не зна́ю,	nait, soòdar, ya yévò nai znàyou.
Where is he?	Гдѣ онъ?	gdai on?
Here he is,	Вотъ опъ,	vott on.
Who is there?	Кто тамъ?	khto tam?
It is I,	Я здѣсь,	ya zdaiss.
I wish to go to the bazar,	Я хочу́ итти́ въ гости́ный дворъ,	ya khatchoò eetteè v' ghasteènee dvor.
What do you wish to buy?	Что изво́лите поку́пать? (что покупа́ете?)	shto eezvòleetee pakoopàt? (shto pakoopàyaitai).
How much does this cost?	Что (мно́го ли) э́то сто́итъ?	shto (mnògo lee) aìto stòeet?
How much do you sell it a pound?	Почему́ фунтъ?	patchaimoò foont?
Five rubles,	Пять рубле́й,	pait roobléy.

I find it very dear,	Э́то, мнѣ ка́жется, о́чень до́рого,	aìto, mnai kàzhaitsa, òtchen dòrogo.
Tell me the lowest price,	Скажи́те мнѣ послѣ́днюю цѣ́ну,	skazheèle mnai paslaìdnyouyou tsaìnoo.
I will not give a higher price,	Я не да́мъ бо́лѣе,	ya nai dam bòlaiyai.
Well, take it!	Хорошо́, изво́льте!	kharashò, eezvòltai!
See, here is your money,	Во́тъ ва́ши де́ньги,	vott vàshee dainghee.
Can you change this bank-note,	Размѣня́йте мнѣ э́ту бума́жку,	razmainyèytai mnai aitoo boomàshkoo.
Give me the balance,	Сда́йте мнѣ оста́льно́е,	zdèytai mnai astalnòyai.
Take that,	Возьми́,	vazmeè.
Give it here,	Пода́й сюда́,	padèy soodà.
Come here, my little friend,	Поди́ сюда́, малю́тка,	padeè soodà, malèwtka.
Here is something for pin-money,	Во́тъ тебѣ́ на була́вки,	vott taibai na boolàfkee.
Tell him to come here,	Позови́ его́ сюда́,	pazaveè yevò soodà.
Tell him I will come,	Скажи́ ему́, что я приду́,	skazheè yemoò shto ya preedoò.
Are you ready?	Гото́вы ли вы?	gatòwee lee wee?
I am very busy,	У меня́ мно́го дѣ́ла,	oo mainà mnògo daìla.
Do you play on the violin?	Игра́ете ли вы на скри́пкѣ?	eegrèytai lee wee na skreèpkai?
No, Miss, I play on the piano,	Извини́те, суда́рыня, я игра́ю на фортепіа́нѣ,	eezveeneèlai, soodàhreena, ya eegràyou na fortepiànai.
I play on the harp,	Я игра́ю на а́рфѣ,	ya eegràyou na àrfai.
I am a great amateur of music,	Я вели́кій охо́тникъ до му́зыки,	ya vaileèkee akhòtneek da moòzeekee.
Don't you play yourself on any instrument?	Не игра́ете ли вы на како́мъ нибу́дь инструме́нтъ?	nai eegràyaitai lee we na kakòm neebòod eenstroomèntai?

I have been too careless,	Я весьма отстал,	ya vaismà atstàll.
Listen!	Послушайте!	paslòohèyte!
Wait a little,	Подождите немного,	padazhdeèlai naimnògo.
It is very early,	Ещё рано,	yeshtchò ràhno.
It is very late,	Ужé поздно,	oozhaì pòzdo.
It 's possible,	Быть можетъ,	bweet mòzhait.
That can not be,	Это быть не можетъ,	aìto bweet nai mòzhait.
It 's understood,	Разумѣется,	razoomaìyetsa.
Do not inconvenience yourself,	Не безпокойтесь,	nai bezpakòytaiss.
That is not your business,	Это не ваше дѣло,	aìto nai vàshai daìlo.
All 's right,	Всё исправлено,	fsyo eespràhvlaino.

Phrases in most common use in familiar conversation.

Tell me, if you please,	Скажите мнѣ, пожалуйста,	skazheètai mnai, pazhàluysta.
Be so kind as to tell me,	Сдѣлайте милость, скажите мнѣ,	zdaìlaytai meèlost, skazheètai mnai.
Excuse me for interrupting you,	Извините, что я перебью вашу рѣчь,	eezveeneètai, shto ya pairaibyoù vàshoo raitch.
I have a favour to ask of you,	Я имѣю до васъ просьбу,	ya eemaìyou da vass pròzboo.
Do not refuse my request,	Не откажите мнѣ въ моей просьбѣ,	nai atkazheètai mnai v' mayèy pròzbai.
You would oblige me very much,	Вы меня очень одолжите,	we mainà òtchen adalzheètai.
Agreed! be it so!	Пусть будетъ такъ!	poost bòdet tak!

66

Willingly. Why not!	Охотно. Для чего жъ не такъ!	akhòtno; dla tchaivòzh nai tak!
With all my heart,	Отъ всего моего сердца,	att fsaivò mayaivò sairtsah.
I am at your disposal,	Я къ вашпмъ услугамъ,	ya k' vàsheem oosloògam.
Rely on me,	Положитесь на меня,	palazheètaiss na mainà.
I am exceedingly obliged to you,	Я вамъ чрезвычайно обязанъ,	ya vam tchraizweetchèyno abàzan.
You are very kind,	Вы очень милостивы,	we òtchen meèlosteewee.
I gratefully accept it,	Я принимаю это съ благодарностью.	ya preeneemàyou aìto s' blagadarnostyou.
You anticipate my wishes,	Вы предупреждаете мои желанія,	we praidoopraizhdàyetai maheè zhailàneeyah.
It's impossible for me,	Это для меня невозможно,	aìto dla mainà naivazmòzhno.
I am sorry for it, but I can't do it,	Я это охотно бы сдѣлалъ, но не могу,	ya aìto akhòtno bwee zdaìlall, no nai magoò.
It grieves me to be obliged to refuse,	Душевно жалѣю, что я долженъ вамъ въ этомъ отказать,	dooshaìvno zhailaìyou, shto ya dòlzhain vam v' aìtom atkazàt.
It will be for another opportunity,	Въ другое время,	v' droogòyai vraìma.
Your servant, do not mention it,	Слуга покорный! этому не бывать,	sloogàh pakòrnee! aìtomoo nai bwevat.
Do not be displaised,	Не прогнѣвайтесь,	nai pragnaivèytaiss.
Do not be angry with me on that account,	Не сердитесь за это на меня,	nai sairdeètaiss za aìto na mainà.
I beg of you not to require it of me,	Пожалуйста, уволльте меня отъ этого,	pazhàluysta, oovòltai mainà att aìtava.
Without ceremony!	Безъ церемоній!	bez tsairaimònee!

Without any compliments!	Безъ комплпмéнтовъ!	bez kompleemèntof!
Familiarly,	Нó-прóсту,	pò-prastoo.
Welcome!	Добрó пожáловать,	dabrò pazhàlovat!
I congratulate you,	Поздравляю вáсъ,	pazdravlàyoo vass.
I am very happy to see you in good health,	Я радъ видя васъ въ дóбромъ здорóвьѣ,	ya rad veéda vass v' dòbrom zdaroveeyai.
Present my respects to him (to her),	Засвидѣ́тельствуйте емý (ей) моё почтéніе,	zasveedaitelstvuytai yemoò(yèy)mayò patchtaineeyai.
Compliment him in my name,	Поклонитесь емý отъ меня,	paklaneètaiss yemoò all mainà.
It is the truth,	Да, э́то прáвда,	da, aito pràvdah.
It is a fact,	Э́то справедлйвое дѣ́ло,	aito spravaidleèvoyai dailo.
You may believe me,	Вы мнѣ мóжете въ томъ повѣ́рить,	we nnnai mòzhaitai f'tom pavaireet.
Be convinced of it,	Бýдьте увѣ́рены,	boòdtai oovairainee.
This gentleman can bear witness to it,	Вотъ Господинъ томý свидѣ́тель,	voll gaspadeèn tamoò sveedaitel.
Undoubtedly,	Безспóрно,	bezspòrno.
You are right,	Вáша прáвда,	vàsha pràvda.
You are not wrong,	Вы справедлйвы (прáвы),	we spravaidleewee (pràhwee).
I do not lie,	Я не лгý,	ya nai lgoo.
I answer for it,	Я вамъ въ томъ ручáюсь,	ya vam f'tom rootchàyouss.
Every body will tell you so,	Это вамъ всякъ скáжетъ,	aito vam fsak skàzhait.
I certify it,	Я вамъ божýсь въ томъ,	ya vam bazhoòss f'tom.
On my honour,	По чéсти!	pa tchaìstee!
As I am an honest man,	Чéстью увѣряю вáсъ,	tchaistyou oovairàyou vass.
Upon my honour,	Чéстное моё слóво,	tchaìssnoyai mayò slòvo.
That is false,	Э́то ложь,	aito losh.

5*

68

Nonsense, idle words,	Э'то пустóе,	aito poostòyai.
That can not be,	Это не мóжетъ стáться,	aito nai mòzhait stàtsa.
No such thing,	Это совсѣмъ пустóе,	aito safsaim poostòyai.
I wager the contrary,	Я бьюсь объ заклáдъ, что не такъ,	ya byouss ob zaklàd, shto nai tak.
You are mistaken,	Вы ошибáетесь,	we asheebàyaitaiss.
Is it in earnest?	Въ сáмомъ ли дѣлѣ?	f' sàmom lee dailai?
Do you speak seriously?	Въ прáвду ли вы говорúте?	v' pràvdoo lee we gavareètai?
Are you not mistaken?	Не ошибáетесь ли вы?	nai asheebàyaitaiss lee we?
I doubt of it,	Я въ э́томъ сомпѣвáюсь,	ya f'tom samnaivàyouss.
I don't believe a word of it,	Я э́тому не вѣрю,	ya aitamoo nai vairoo.
You jest,	Вы шýтите,	we shoòteetai.
It's not to be believed,	Э'то невѣроя́тно,	aito naivairayàtno.
It's incomprehensible,	Это непоня́тно,	aito naipanàtno.
They have deceived you,	Васъ э́тимъ обманýли,	vass aiteem abmanoòlee.
That is beyond my comprehension,	Это вы́ше моегó поня́тія,	aito weèshai mayevò panàteeya.
What do you say?	Что вы говорúте?	shto we gavareètai?
Of what do you speak?	О чёмъ вы говорúте?	ah tchom we gavareètai?
What do you want?	Чегó желáете?	tchaivò zhailàyaitai?
What's to be done?	Что тутъ остаётся дѣлать?	shto toot astayòtsa dàilat?
What do you think of it?	Какъ вы объ э́томъ посýдите?	kak we ab aitom passoodeètai?
What do you advise me to do?	Что вы мнѣ присовѣтуете?	shto we mnai preessavaitooyaitai?
How can we help it?	Какъ э́тому пособúть?	kak aitamoo passabeèt?

What is your advice?	Какое ваше мнѣніе?	kakòvai vàshai muainyai?
Would it not be better to....?	Не лучше ли будетъ?	nai lootchai lce boòdait?
Where are you going?	Куда вы идёте?	koodàh wec eedyòtai?
I am going to...,	Я иду въ ... (къ),	ya eedoò v'...(k').
I have just gone out of your house,	Я иду отъ васъ,	ya eedoò at vass.
I am going home,	Я возвращаюсь домой,	ya vazvrashtchàyouss damòy.
Rest yourself a little,	Отдохните немного,	atdakneétai nemnògo.
Remain there,	Останьтесь здѣсь,	astàntess zdaiss.
Return shortly,	Возвратитесь скорѣе,	vazvrateèless skarèy.
Be not long before you return,	Не умедлите возвратиться,	nai oomaidleetai vazvrateètsa.
Come up,	Всходите,	fskhadeètai.
Go down.	Сойдите,	seydeétai.
Draw back a little,	Подвиньтесь немного,	padveéntaiss naimnògo.
Depart,	Отойдите,	ateydeétai.
Clear the way,	Посторопитесь,	pastaraneètaiss.
Let me pass,	Дайте мнѣ пройти,	dèytai mnai preytteè.
Be gone!	Идите прочь!	eedeètai protch.
Be off!	Убирайся!	oobeerèysa.
Speak reasonably,	Говорите дѣло,	gavareètai dàilo.
You talk at random,	Вы болтаете безъ разбора,	wee ballàyaitai baiz razbòra.
Let us chat a little,	Поговоримъ немного,	pagavareèm naimnògo.
You split my head,	Вы мнѣ вскружили голову,	wee mnai fskroozheèlee gòlovoo.
Be silent!	Молчите!	maltcheètai.
Hush! silence!	Стъ! Молчать!	st! maltchàt!
How beautiful it is!	Вотъ это прекрасно!	vott aìto praikràsno!

Marvellously!	Превосхо́дно!	praivaskhòdno!
It's astonishing,	Э́то удиви́тельно,	aito oodeeveètailno.
I am astonished at it,	Я э́тому удивля́юсь,	ya aitamoo odeevlàyouss.
It is a very surprizing thing,	Э́то удиви́тельная вещь,	aito oodeeveètailnayah vaistch.
What a pleasure!	Како́е удово́льствіе!	kakòyai oodavòlstvyai!
How happy I am!	Какъ я дово́ленъ!	kak ya davòlain!
What unexpected happiness!	Како́е вечя́нное благополу́чіе!	kakòyai naitchàyannoyai blagopaloòtchyai!
I am wearied,	Мнѣ ску́чпо,	mnai skoòshno.
I am sad,	Я раздоса́дованъ,	ya razdassàdovann.
How unhappy I am!	Какъ я несчя́стенъ!	kak ya naistchàstain!
What a disappointment,	Кака́я неуда́ча!	kakàya naioodàtcha!
Every thing tends to thwart me to-day,	Во всёмъ мнѣ сего́дня препя́тствіе,	va fsyom mnai saivòdnee praipyàtsvyai.
I am grieved,	Я въ отчя́яніи,	ya v' atchàyanee,
All is lost,	Все пропа́ло,	fsio prapàhlo.
We must take patience,	Должно́ потерпѣ́ть,	dalzhnò potairpait.
Have patience for a little time,	Потерпи́те ещё немно́го,	patairpeètai yeshtchò naimnògo.
Take heart,	Ободри́тесь,	abadreètaiss.
For God's sake!	Ра́ди Бо́га!	ràdee bòha!
Heaven grant it!	Дай Богъ!	dey bokh!
God forbid!	Не дай Богъ!	nai dey bokh!
Heaven forefend!	Изба́ви Бо́же!	eezbàvee bòzhai!
Please God!	Е́сли такъ уго́дно Бо́гу,	yèslee tak oogòdno bòhoo.
Help!	Помоги́те!	pamagheètai!

COMPARATIVE TABLE
OF COINS, WEIGHTS AND MEASURES
OF RUSSIA AND ENGLAND.

COINS.	ESTIMATION			
	IN RUSSIAN COINS.		IN ENGLISH COINS.	
IN GOLD.	Rubles.	Ko-pecs.	Shil-lings.	Pence.
The imperial (имперіалъ) . . .	10	—	33	6
The half-imperial (полуимперіалъ)	5	—	16	9
The ducat (червóнецъ)	3	—	9	7
IN SILVER.			s.	d.
The ruble (рубль)	—	100	3	1
The half-ruble (полтѝшникъ) . .	—	50	1	7
The quarter of ruble (четвертáкъ) .	—	25	—	10
The piece of 20 kopecs (двугрѝвеннпкъ)	—	20	—	8
The piece of 15 kopecs (злóтый)	—	15	—	6
The piece of 10 kopecs (грѝвенникъ)	—	10	—	4
The piece of 5 kopecs (пятáкъ) .	—	5	—	2
IN COPPER.			Penco.	Far-things.
The piece of 3 kopecs (трикопѣечникъ)	—	3	—	5
The grosh (грошъ)	—	2	—	3 1/5
The kopec (копѣйка)	—	1	—	1 3/5
The deneshka (дѐнежка) . . .	—	1/2	—	4/5
The poloòshka (полýшка) . . .	—	1/4	—	2/5

WEIGHTS.	ESTIMATION			
	IN RUSSIAN WEIGHTS.		IN ENGLISH WEIGHTS.	
	Pounds	Zolot-neeks.	Avoir du pois Pounds	Ounces
The bèrkovets (бéрковецъ) . . .	400	—	361	—
The pood (пудъ)	40	—	36	10
The pound (фунтъ)	—	96	—	$14\tfrac{1}{2}$
The lot (лотъ)	—	3	—	$7\tfrac{7}{16}$
The zolotneèk (золотнúкъ) . . .	—	1	—	$7\tfrac{7}{48}$
The zolotneèk is divided into 96 дóли	—	—	—	—

MEASURES.	ESTIMATION			
	IN RUSSIAN MEASURES.		IN ENGLISH MEASURES.	
LONG MEASURES.	Feet.	Inches.	Yards.	Feet.
The verst (верстá) has 500 sazhèns .	3500	—	1166	2
The sazhèn (сажéнь) has 3 arsheens	7	—	2	1
			Feet.	Inches.
The arsheèn(apшúнъ)has 16 vorshòks	2	4	2	4
The vershòk (вершóкъ)	—	$1\tfrac{3}{4}$	—	$1\tfrac{3}{4}$
The foot (футъ)	—	12	1	—
The inch (дюймъ) has 12 lines .	—	1	—	1

SQUARE MEASURES.	Square sazhèns.	Acres.	Roods
The desseteèna (десятúна) . . .	2400	2	2

SOLID MEASURES.	Cubic feet.	Cords.
The cubic sazhèn (кубúческая сажéнь)	343	$2\tfrac{7}{10}$

LIQUID MEASURES.	ESTIMATION			
	IN RUSSIAN MEASURES.		IN ENGLISH MEASURES.	
	Ve-dros.	Kroo-shki.	Gal-lons.	Quarts.
The tun (бóчка)	40	—	109	1
The anker (áнкерокъ)	3	—	8	$4\frac{1}{5}$
The vedro (ведрó)	—	10	2	$2\frac{1}{5}$
The kroòshka (крýжка) has 10 чáрки	—	1	—	1

DRY MEASURES.	Tchet-vereeks	Gar-nets.	Gal-lons.	Quarts.
The kool (куль)	10	—	55	3
The tchètvert (чéтверть) . . .	8	—	44	—
The osmeèna (осьмúна)	4	—	22	—
The tchetvereèk (четверíкъ) . .	—	8	5	2
The half-tchetvereèk (получетве-рíкъ)	—	4	2	3
The tchetvyòrtka (четвёртка) . .	—	2	1	$1\frac{1}{2}$
The gàrnets (гáрнецъ)	—	1	—	$2\frac{3}{4}$
The half-gàrnets (полугáрнецъ) .	—	$\frac{1}{2}$	—	$1\frac{3}{8}$

CONTENTS.

www.ingramcontent.com/pod-product-compliance
Lightning Source LLC
Chambersburg PA
CBHW021526270326
41930CB00008B/1107